Radical Discipleship

Radical Discipleship
Reflections on the Sermon on the Mount

ROLAND CHIA

Eugene, Oregon

RADICAL DISCIPLESHIP
Reflections on the Sermon on the Mount

Copyright © 2006 Roland Chia. All rights reserved. Except for brief quotations in critical articles or reviews, no part of this book may be reproduced in any manner without prior written permission from the publisher. Write: Permissions, Wipf and Stock Publishers, 199 W. 8th Ave., Suite 3, Eugene, OR 97401.

ISBN: 1-59752-525-1

Cataloging-in-Publication Data

Chia, Roland, 1960–

  Radical discipleship : reflections on the sermon on the mount / Roland Chia.

xii + 110 p.; 20 cm.

Includes bibliographical references.

ISBN 1-59752-525-1   (alk. paper)

1. Sermon on the Mount—Theology. 2. Christian life—Biblical teaching. I. Title.

BT380.2 C710 2006

Manufactured in the U.S.A.

Contents

Preface / ix

CHAPTER ONE: **The Way of the Disciple / 1**

The Beatitudes (Matthew 5:3-12) / 1

Salt and Light (Matthew 5:13-16) / 7

CHAPTER TWO: **Ethics of the Kingdom I / 12**

Jesus, the Christian and the Law (Matthew 5:17-20) / 12

On Murder (Matthew 5:21-26) / 16

Avoiding Lust (Matthew 5:27-30) / 19

CHAPTER THREE: **Ethics of the Kingdom II / 24**

Concerning Divorce (Matthew 5:31-32) / 24

Concerning Credibility (Matthew 5:33-37) / 28

Turning the Other Cheek (Matthew 5:38-42) / 32

Loving Our Enemies (Matthew 5:43-48) / 36

CHAPTER FOUR: **On Love and Piety / 41**

Parading Piety (Matthew 6:1-4) / 41

On Prayer and Performance (Matthew 6:5-8) / 44

Hidden Spirituality (Matthew 6:16-18) / 48

CHAPTER FIVE: **The Lord's Prayer I / 52**

Our Father Who Art in Heaven (Matthew 6:9a) / 52

Hallowed Be Thy Name (Matthew 6:9b) / 55

Thy Kingdom Come (Matthew 6:10) / 60

CHAPTER SIX: **The Lord's Prayer II / 65**

Our Daily Bread (Matthew 6:11) / 65

Forgive Us Our Sins (Matthew 6:12a) / 69

And Lead Us Not Into Temptation (Matthew 6:13) / 72

Deliver Us from Evil (Matthew 6:13b) / 76

CHAPTER SEVEN: **On Seeking First the Kingdom / 81**

Money Matters Matter (Matthew 6:19-24) / 81

Seeking the Kingdom (Matthew 6:25-34) / 85

On Judging Others (Matthew 7:1-6) / 88

Ask, Seek and Knock (Matthew 7:7-12) / 92

CHAPTER EIGHT: **Sure Foundation / 96**

The Narrow Gate of Salvation (Matthew 7:13-14) / 96

A Tree and Its Fruit (Matthew 7:15-23) / 100

Two Builders (Matthew 7:24-29) / 104

Bibliography / 109

Preface

THE SERMON on the Mount is probably the most famous passage in the Gospel of Matthew. Even unbelievers like Mahatma Gandhi appreciate the teaching of the Sermon and applaud the high morality that it advocates. Phrases like "love your enemies" and "turn the other cheek" are also frequently used in public discourse, even though they are sometimes quoted to mock the idealistic morality of Christianity. Others have found in some statements of the beatitudes, like "Blessed are the peacemakers, for they shall be called sons of God," a powerful rhetoric in this world of war, violence, terrorism, and bloodshed.

Familiarity with the Sermon on the Mount, however, can ironically prevent us from understanding its true message. This is true for the Christian as well, as he or she is exposed to popular and sometimes profoundly misleading interpretations of these chapters in the Gospel of Matthew. In order to understand the meaning of the Sermon, we must ask fundamental questions like, What is the main focus of the Sermon? Is this Sermon primarily about morality, as many of its interpreters seem to suggest? Does it present ethical principles to which all Christians must submit? Or is the Sermon indicative of the attitude and conduct of a new community under the reign of God, which Jesus Christ has come to inaugurate? Put differently, does the Sermon on the Mount present an ideal morality or does it present the dawn of a new reality of which the disciples of Christ are already a part?

This book is written with the firm conviction that the Sermon on the Mount cannot be reduced to a morality, a set of ethical principles for Christians. It is not the Christian equivalent of, say, the Analects of Confucius. To be sure, the Sermon does make rigorous moral demands on those who claim to be followers of Christ. But the Sermon also announces, together with the rest of the Gospel of Matthew; that, with the coming of the incarnate Son of God in Jesus Christ, a new reality has dawned. God's kingdom has broken into human history, and a new people have been called into being; they are already partakers of the new life that Christ has made possible. The Sermon presents the attitude, values, and conduct of the new community that Christ has gathered in his name. These values are not only inimical to that of the world, but are, indeed, antithetical to them.

But the new reality, which has already dawned in human history, awaits its final consummation. The ambivalence of the "already" and the "not yet" is therefore evident throughout the Sermon, as it calls the followers of Christ and citizens of the kingdom of God to a radical discipleship in a fallen world. And it is in light of this ambivalence that the Sermon must be read and understood. The Sermon presents discipleship as an "impossible possibility"! The Sermon on the Mount, therefore, is meaningless if it is read without Christ and the kingdom of God. Without them, the Sermon presents moral ideals that are simply impossible to attain. But in light of Christ and the eschatological kingdom of God, the Sermon gives us a glimpse into what kingdom living is like. Furthermore, when read in light of Christ and the kingdom of God, the Sermon challenges those who are called by his name to be a community of character. It challenges Christians to seek the kingdom and righteousness of God before all else and above all else.

This book began life as a series of monthly reflections published in the *Methodist Message*, the official newsletter of the Methodist Church in Singapore. I would like to thank the editor, Peter Teo, for inviting me to contribute to the publication and for permission to republish the articles in this form. I would also like to thank the bishop of the Methodist Church in Singapore, Dr. Robert Solomon, for encouraging me to publish this exposition for readers beyond the Methodist community in Singapore.

CHAPTER ONE

The Way of the Disciple

The Beatitudes (Matthew 5:3-12)

THE FIRST section of the Sermon (vv. 3-12), commonly called the Beatitudes, boldly promises happiness or blessedness to the citizens of the kingdom proclaimed by Jesus. Matthew has nine beatitudes, of which the first four will be discussed in this section. The subject of the first beatitude is the "poor in spirit," This phrase describes an attitude. And so, while the phrase may include those who suffer from material poverty, it does not refer *only* or even *primarily* to them. This point must be made in the face of modern interpretations of this beatitude, especially by liberation theologians, that appear to privilege the poor and canonize poverty. Their approach has led them to the claim that the poor are the epiphany of the Kingdom. Against this interpretation it must be remembered that this statement describes an attitude, one that even the poor may not possess. The poor described in this beatitude are not those living below the poverty line, but God's poor—those who are totally dependent on God; those who continue to trust in God although they are persecuted and oppressed because of their faith. These belong to the kingdom of God. God's poor are heirs of every spiritual wealth that his kingdom holds.

The second beatitude is for those who mourn. Again, the reference is to the downtrodden disciples of Christ. The promise of the beatitude echoes the prophecy of Isaiah that the Messiah will come to "comfort all those who mourn" (Isaiah 61:2). The attitude described here is alive only to those who possess character and substance. The mourners are those who are able to see the depths of the plight of humanity. They grieve over sin and evil—whether their own or that of others. They identify with the oppressed, the disenfranchised, and the marginalized. They cry out against the injustices in the world and mourn in the face of evil. They pray daily that God will act and bring about his justice—that he will punish the wicked and vindicate the righteous. They pray daily, "Thy will be done, on earth as it is in heaven." They mourn, but the beatitude makes clear that one day their mourning will cease, for they will be comforted by the God of all comforts. The comfort they seek is nothing short of the eschatological realization of reign of God in the world. In the end, their prayers will be answered, for their travail has not escaped the notice of God.

The third beatitude has to do with the meek. Meekness is not weakness. The world regards the two as synonyms; but, in the great reversal of the world's values, the Sermon presents meekness as the mark of maturity and strength of character. Meekness means humility before God and gentleness before man. It must not be understood as submissiveness due to lack of resources, ingenuity, or courage. Meekness is, rather, temperance and self-control; it is the quality that belongs to those who could assert themselves, but choose not to do so for the sake of the kingdom. In this sense, meekness marks true strength of character, exposing arrogance, aggression, and violence as cowardice and as crass immaturity. Meekness triumphs in the end, for those who exhibit this quality will inherit the earth. Again one must be careful not to read this as a form of Taoist philosophy of non-action: "that weakness will prevail over strength and that gentleness will conquer the adamant hindrance of men" (*Tao te Ching*).

Christians are not called to be passive. Christians are called to the world to proclaim the Gospel, and an essential character of this proclamation is the embodiment in their lives of the principle and the ethic of the Gospel. But what must be remembered is that the triumph of the meek here is, in the end, the triumph of God and his eschatological kingdom. This is a triumph that is won by Christ on the Cross. The meek will, in the end, "possess the land." And this land will be the coming messianic kingdom, in which the wicked tyrants and bullies of this world shall have no place.

The fourth beatitude speaks of those who hunger and thirst for righteousness. The righteousness for which they hunger and thirst is the righteousness of God. Thus, it is a given righteousness and not one that can be achieved by our own efforts. The blessed are those who hunger and thirst for it, and they will be filled. To repeat, it is God who will, in the end, satisfy them with his righteousness. Again, this does not argue for passivity. Surely, those who hunger and thirst for righteousness must themselves be seeking to live righteous lives. Surely too, they must want to do their level best, as their basic responsibility to society, to fight injustice and expose evil. But they do so not to "change society" as such and so bring forth an earthly utopia, for it is not within their power to do this. They do so simply because they hunger and thirst for righteousness and because they serve a righteous God. And as they walk in obedience to this righteous God, they fulfill their calling as the light of the world and salt of the earth.

With the next beatitude a new emphasis is made. Whereas the first four beatitudes are concerned with the state of mind and inner disposition of the disciple, the fifth emphasizes the blessings that result from his conduct, from his direct act towards his neighbor. *Blessed are the merciful, for they will be shown mercy.* To be merciful is to forgive the guilty and to show compassion to the suffering and the needy.

Mercy requires us to step outside of our own comfort zones and secure environments to reach out to the other. Mercy always demands that we extend ourselves towards others, which means that an act of mercy may cause discomfort and disruption in our own lives. Mercy cannot take place in stoic detachment but only in genuine identification. And identification with the other may mean that one must be willing to sacrifice what is perhaps the greatest treasure of human life—one's dignity and honor—for the sake of the other. It was mercy that compelled Jesus to suffer humiliation and death on the Cross for the sake of the other. Those who show mercy in this way will in turn receive mercy from God, the merciful One. Here the reward serves also as an important reminder—those who show mercy are themselves in need of mercy. It is precisely because the disciple is fully conscious of the fact that he is a sinner in need of the mercy of God that he is compelled to be merciful towards others.

Blessed are the pure in heart, for they shall see God. Purity of heart is constantly required of God's people in Scripture. In Psalm 24:3-4 we read: "Who may ascend the hill of the Lord? Who may stand in his holy place? He who has clean hands and a pure heart." The phrase "pure in heart" describes the inner core of a person, his thoughts and motivations. It assumes right actions, but penetrates deeper, beneath the surface into the very essence of the person, and exposes his spiritual condition. Right actions may well be done with impure motives. Benevolent acts may be performed for selfish gains. Exteriors may deceive. This beatitude penetrates beneath the exterior to the very core and works its way from inside out, as it were. It reaches the heart of the disciple, a place where only God can reach. Perhaps here is an anticipation of Jesus' diatribe against the Pharisees and religious leaders of his day, whose outward religiosity and piety contradicted the condition of their hearts. The pure in heart do not live in this contradiction. In fact, the pure in heart are focused and single-minded. Their desire is to serve the Lord and to imitate their Master. They surrender every selfish desire, every impure thought, every hidden motive, to the sanctifying grace of God, and seek to live in perfect obedience to God. Those who are pure in heart will receive the beatific vision—they will see the face of God.

The next beatitude concerns peacemakers. Peace is a theme that is found in both testaments. The disciples of Christ are called to be peacemakers and thus to testify to the kingdom of peace, which the Messiah, the Prince of Peace, will eventually bring about. The beatitude does not specify the different situations in which peacemaking occurs and therefore must be applied generally and quite universally, from making peace between two warring nations to making peace in a quarrel between two individuals. Notice also here that disciples are called to be peace*makers*, not just peace*keepers*. The latter is somewhat more passive, involving a general disinclination to engage in disputes. This is, of course, admirable and must surely be the concern of every disciple of Christ, especially in a world that is rife with quarrels, hatred, strife, bitterness, and pettiness. But the beatitude speaks of a more active role that the disciple must play, that of *making* peace. Again, this involves extending oneself to the other, for peacemaking cannot take place when we refuse to care about others. Peacemaking, which is synonymous to the ministry of reconciliation, cannot be accomplished by remote control or at arm's length—it requires nothing less than entering the arena of conflict.

Peace in our world is costly. Jesus came to bring peace—peace between God and man and peace between man and man—and he had to pour out his life in order to accomplish his purpose. The same may be true of the disciple. For peace must be distinguished from appeasement and from the diplomacy that we are so accustomed to find in a culture fraught with the rhetoric of political correctness.

True peace can never be achieved without Truth; and in this sinful world, Truth often divides, for there will always be those who prefer falsehood. Thus, in this and all the beatitudes, the eschatological dimension can never be marginalized. True peace can only come with the consummation of the kingdom. But the children of God, who live by faith in the here and now, must be peacemakers and so bear witness to the kingdom, which has already come and which will be manifested in fullness at the end of time.

The paradoxes that we encounter in the beatitudes reach their climax in the final beatitude: *Blessed are those who are persecuted because of righteousness, for theirs is the kingdom of God.* It is significant that this beatitude comes just after the one concerning peacemaking. It confirms our argument that peace is not to be attained at all cost and at the expense of Truth. Here in this beatitude, those who are called to be peacemakers will also be the ones who will be persecuted. They who work for peace will themselves experience no peace, because there will be those who would try to silence them. This is because the peace that they wish to bring about is inextricably related to righteousness—not their own, but God's. They are persecuted because they hunger and thirst for this righteousness and because they seek to walk in the way of the Lord. Since Christ is the righteousness of God, those who would follow Christ must expect persecution from anti-God forces. The disciples will suffer insults and slander just as their Lord and Master suffered.

The paradox is that they are told to rejoice while under persecution—to respond with exuberant joy. It must be emphasized that we do not have here a morbidity or the kind of "persecution syndrome" that we witness in some cults. The disciples of Christ do not rejoice because of the persecution, but because of the reward that awaits them. This reward is in heaven, and therefore points not only to the future but also to the otherworldly. It is a reward for their faithfulness and perseverance, for their commitment and devotion. It must also be emphasized that the reward here is the result of God's grace. It is God who rewards those whom he preserves and protects.

Are the Beatitudes nothing but a splendid example of supra-moral idealism? Is the spirituality that they describe achievable at all? *Can* the disciples accomplish what they *ought* to? To be sure, the spirituality of the Beatitudes does present an ideal for which all the disciples of Christ must strive. But this striving itself, it must be remembered, is a striving that is enabled by the grace of God. The Beatitudes, therefore, would truly be impossible if not for grace. That is why, at the outset, I stressed that the Beatitudes, and indeed the Sermon of the Mount as a whole, cannot be read from any other standpoint except the Christological. It cannot be understood apart from the grace of God, which is found through union with Christ. By the grace of God in Christ, the impossible demands of the Beatitudes, and, indeed, of the Sermon on the Mount, become possible. Theologically, the Beatitudes can only be understood within the larger framework of the doctrine of sanctification.

Salt and Light (Matthew 5:13-16)

This passage that immediately follows the Beatitudes makes it unequivocally clear that election and responsibility are profoundly related. The disciples of Christ, whose spirituality is portrayed in the Beatitudes, have a responsibility towards the corrupt and dark world from which they are set apart and to which they are called to proclaim the Good News. So if the Beatitudes spoke of the blessedness of the disciples, this section of the Sermon drives home their responsibility. It provides "kingdom" ethics that the disciples of Christ are expected to embody as they go about their business and attend to day-to-day affairs. In their existence and being in the world, the disciples of Christ are to be "salt of the earth" and "light of the world." The emphatic "you yourselves" at the beginning of verses 13 and 14 stresses the precedence of being over doing: this is who they are; they are salt and light. Their behavior, therefore, must correspond to their identity if they are to live authentically in the world and bear the name Christian.

The first metaphor that is used to describe the disciples is "salt." This metaphor has generated quite a spirited debate among scholars: what exactly did Jesus intend to say by this metaphor? Which quality of salt did he have in mind? Several have been suggested: preservation, purification, seasoning, even fertilization. None, however, appear to be fully adequate. The problem is made more difficult with the joining of two metaphors in the sentence: "You are the *salt* of the *earth*." But salt has no beneficial effect upon soil. Of course, this difficulty could be resolved by reminding ourselves that this metaphor is not based on modern science but on a common practice during the time of Jesus. And salt was used as fertilizer in the ancient world.

A more serious problem is the latter statement: "But if salt loses its saltiness, how can it be made salty again?" Sodium chloride is a chemically stable compound—it does not lose its saltiness. But this statement has a proverbial character. Furthermore, some scholars think that the reference here is probably to the salt cakes that are taken from the Dead Sea and extracted through evaporation. In this case, salt will be mixed with other minerals mistaken for salt and therefore deemed to have lost its saltiness. These difficulties aside, the meaning of this statement is quite clear. Just as salt is vitally important to everyday life, so the disciples were necessary and significant to the world in their proclamation of the kingdom and in their embodiment of kingdom ethics.

The next metaphor is "light." Again, the emphatic "you yourselves" places stress on the disciples' identity. The phrase "light of the world" implies that the world is in darkness, and darkness in Scripture always refers to sin. Light is, of course, a very significant metaphor in Scripture, used supremely for Christ himself. In John 8:12 Jesus said: "I am the Light of the world. Whoever follows me will never walk in darkness, but will have the light of life" (See also John 9:5). In the Sermon, Jesus transferred this metaphor to his disciples, the Church. Thus the Church is the light of the world only in a derivative sense. The Church bears no light of her own, but reflects the Light of Christ as she walks in obedience to her Lord. Christians are, therefore, "the children of light" (Ephesians 5:8; 1 Thess 5:5) and are called to "shine as lights" in the darkness of this fallen world (Philippians 2:15) just as the people of Israel were called to be the "light to the Gentiles" (Isaiah 51:4-5). Thus, the light of the church is the reflection of the Light of God made manifest in Christ.

A city on a hill cannot be hidden from sight; no one lights a lamp only to hide it under a bowl. He will hang the lighted lamp on a stand so that those in the house would benefit from it. The stress here is on the visibility of the Church. She cannot be hidden from public view and therefore has the potential to influence the wider culture, whether she realizes it or not. The idea of the closet Christian is here refuted as ridiculous, as ridiculous as hiding a lit lamp under a bowl. The Church exists in a larger environment, the public domain. This is a fact, and the Church (and therefore individual Christians) cannot escape the public eye. Thus, the injunction is to match one's identity with one's behavior: "Let your light shine before men, that they may see your good deeds and praise your Father in heaven."

This is the climax of the section. Christians are to let their light shine before men by living in such a way that the presence of the kingdom is made manifest. They are to embody the spirituality of the Beatitudes and so be the salt of the earth and the light of the world that they are meant to be. The emphasis on "good works" must be given some attention. Good works, properly understood, are always the result of one's faith in God. Thus, good works are expected of the citizens of the kingdom—it must be remembered that Jesus is here speaking about his disciples—they are not that which qualifies people for the kingdom. But as we read further in the Sermon, we find a very specific instruction for the disciples *not* to do their good works before people (see Matthew 6:1-6). Is there a contradiction between Matthew 5:16 and 6:1? The answer is that there is no contradiction, for the difference between them lies in motivation. In Matthew 6:1 Jesus spoke against the Pharisees and religious leaders who perform good works *for their own self-glorification*. But, as the latter part of the verse makes clear, in Matthew 5:16 the good works that are wrought by the disciples should point beyond themselves to God. The final result is that onlookers will "see your good deeds and praise your Father in heaven."

The Church has not always been true to her calling to be salt of the earth and light of the world. There are many dark episodes in her long history that bear witness to this fact. One need only to think of the Crusades of the eleventh and twelfth centuries, the Inquisitions of the Middles Ages, and the countless of atrocities that the Church is either party to or acquiesce in: the slave-trade in the seventeenth century; anti-Semitism in Romania, Russia, and Germany; Apartheid in South Africa. These were moments when the Church had lost her saltiness and her light had dimmed. They were also occasions when the church had sought to walk her own way, to rely upon the integrity of her own reasoning, to form her own judgments on the basis of her evaluation of the empirical facts, and to rely on the words of men rather than on the Word of God. Put differently, those dark moments of the

Church's history point to her disobedience, her pride of reason, and her sense of self-sufficiency. The Sermon warns us against this. The Church can only be salt and light when she embodies the spirituality of the Beatitudes, when she understands that she is the community of the Crucified. She will be salt and light only when her righteousness transcends that of the religious culture of her day and when her spirituality is vivified by the Crucified One.

CHAPTER TWO

Ethics of the Kingdom I

Jesus, the Christian, and the Law (Matthew 5:17-20)

JESUS NOW turns to the law and clarifies his relationship to it. There are notable movements as the Sermon progresses. Jesus began his Sermon with the beatitudes in the third person ("Blessed are the poor in spirit"); he continues in the second person as he addresses his disciples ("You are the salt of the earth"); and now he moves to the authoritative first person ("I say to you" [v. 18], "I tell you" [v. 20]). His opening statement suggests that some of his hearers were of the opinion that he had come to abolish ("destroy") the law. This may have been true especially of the Pharisees and religious leaders, who felt that the radical and unorthodox ways in which Jesus interpreted the Law must signal the latter's desire to abolish it. "Law" here refers to the entire Torah, not only to the first five books of the Hebrew Scriptures. This is made clear by the Matthean addition of "the Prophets." Thus, "Law" refers to the Old Testament in its entirety. Jesus emphatically denied that he has come to destroy or annul the Word of God in the Old Testament. Rather he maintained that he had come to *fulfill* it.

It is vitally important that this assertion is properly understood. The Greek word, which the NIV rendered as "fulfill," can be variously translated as "accomplish," "complete,"

Ethics of the Kingdom I 13

"bring to completion," "finish," or even "fill." It would be a mistake, however, to think that by this Jesus meant that he has come simply to add something to the law. The full weight of the statement cannot be appreciated only through word study. The meaning of the statement can be ascertained only by examining it in the light of the entire passage and its subsequent applications in 5:21-48.

"Torah" means "revealed instruction." The Old Testament contains doctrinal teaching regarding God, man, and salvation. Jesus Christ is the fulfillment in the sense that, as God Incarnate, he is the supreme revelation of God and of his will. But the Old Testament also contains predictive prophecies about the coming Messiah. These prophecies were fulfilled in the Person of Jesus Christ. And finally, the Old Testament contains ethical precepts. These precepts are embodied in the Person of Jesus Christ, who is the revelation of the righteousness of God. Thus, the context suggests that Jesus Christ accomplishes the Law not just by supplementing it, but by bringing out its fullest meaning and significance. Put differently, *when Jesus Christ said that he is the fulfillment of the law, he meant that the meaning and significance of the law can only be fully understood in the light of who he is.* So John 5:39: "You diligently study the Scriptures because you think that by them you possess eternal life. These are the Scriptures that testify about me, yet you refuse to come to me and have life."

Only when we accept this are we able to understand the full significance of the ensuing passages in the rest of the chapter. In a sense, this declaration prepares the reader for the controversial passages that deal with murder, adultery, divorce, oaths, revenge, and the nature of Christian love. They are controversial not only because of their subject matter, but also because of their presentation. Jesus used the formula "You have heard that it was said . . . but I tell you" to begin his discourse on each of the topics. The first part of the formula is commonly used in rabbinic instructions. But the second part of the formula is not only totally unprecedented, but entirely alien to the spirit of the rabbis; for no rabbi would dare pit his view against that of Scripture. Jesus' use of this formula can only be understood in the light of who he is. His teaching, therefore, can only be accepted by those who recognize his true identity.

What about the relationship between the law and the Christian? To his disciples Jesus made this remarkable assertion: "I tell you . . . unless your righteousness surpasses that of the Pharisees and the teachers of the law, you will certainly not enter into the kingdom of heaven." This assertion had doubtless astounded the religious leaders who were present. But it is also shocking to Protestant and evangelical Christians. Is Jesus not implying that salvation is based on works? A Pelagian reading of this passage is certainly possible (Pelagius was a fourth century English monk who taught that man could attain his salvation by obeying the divine law. Augustine of Hippo rejected this teaching, insisting that scripture explicitly teaches that salvation is possible only by grace). But careful exegesis would show that a Pelagian reading of this passage would not be correct.

In the first place, Jesus was talking about a different kind of righteousness from the one pursued and exhibited by the religious leaders. Theirs was a truncated understanding of righteousness that is defined by legalism. They dwelt on the letter of the law and therefore they had simply missed the point. Hence, Jesus could say, somewhat brutally, of the Pharisees: "You give a tenth of your spices—mint, dill and cumin. But you have neglected the more important matters of the law—justice, mercy and faithfulness" (Matthew 23:23). Second, the religious leaders failed to see (or accept) that Jesus is the fulfillment of the law, and that only those who believe in him will receive God's salvation and be made righteous in the sight of God.

Ethics of the Kingdom I 15

The disciples of Christ must be different. They must understand the true meaning of the Word of God. They must understand that their new life in Christ has given them a new standing before God. But this must not lead them to disregard the law. Rather, they must live according to the spirit of the law. They must go beyond the superficial externalities that legalism prescribes and display that true spirituality that images the justice, love, and mercy of God. The righteousness of Jesus' disciples is therefore qualitatively different from that of the religious leaders; it comes only from acknowledging who Jesus is and understanding the true meaning of the Word of God through him. Thus, Jesus was not hinting here that salvation can be achieved through good works. In fact, he was arguing the exact opposite. He was making the point that it is quite impossible to understand, much less attain, righteousness apart from him.

The Christian must avoid the two opposite errors of legalism and antinomianism. To repeat, legalism, as that morbid preoccupation with the letter of the law, prevents one from discovering its real intention. Legalism blinds us from the spirit of the law, its true significance. Antinomianism, on the other hand, is the view that the Christian is not bound by the moral law. Antinomianism is vivified by a false notion of freedom. Both legalism and antinomianism violate the relationship that the Christian has with his Lord, but in different ways. Legalism reduces that relationship to rules and regulations. Antinomianism treats the relationship in a flippant and supercilious fashion.

The true disciple of Christ, because of his relationship with his Lord, understands the true meaning of the law and allows it to shape and mold his character. This is what distinguishes the righteousness of the disciples from that of the Pharisees. As the German theologian Dietrich Bonhoeffer has so eloquently put it, "It is a righteousness under the cross, it belongs only to the poor, the tempted, the hungry, the meek, the peacemakers, the persecuted—who endure their lot for the sake of Jesus; it is the visible righteousness of those who for the sake of Jesus are the light of the world and the city set on the hill. This is where the righteousness of the disciple exceeds that of the Pharisees; it is grounded solely on the call to fellowship with him who alone fulfils the law."

On Murder (Matthew 5:21-26)

The first of the five antitheses in 5:21-42 deals with murder, or, more precisely, anger. Jesus begins with the formula: "You have heard that it was said long ago." This refers to a tradition that his hearers were familiar with, one that was handed down from generation to generation. He then quotes *verbatim* one of the commandments in the Decalogue: "You shall not kill" (See Exodus 20:15 and Deuteronomy 5:18), adding that "anyone who murders will be subjected to judgment." Judgment here refers to both the judgment of the authorities of the religious leaders and that of God. Then, with the formulaic "But I say to you . . . ." Jesus introduces a new dimension to this tradition that must have shocked most of his hearers. To begin with, his approach itself is radical and, to some of his hearers, almost blasphemous. Jesus appears not only to be challenging the received traditions but the Torah itself. Only those who accept who Jesus truly is will be able to accept what he has to say and understand its significance.

"Anyone who is angry with his brother will be subjected to judgement. Again, anyone who says to his brother 'Raca' is answerable to the Sanhedrin. But anyone who says 'You fool!' will be in danger of the fire of hell." According to Jesus, anger is a violation of the law of God and makes the person liable for judgment. For the religious leaders, the sixth commandment prohibits premeditated murder. But Jesus went behind the murderous intention and includes anger—which

Ethics of the Kingdom I 17

may be described as murdering someone in your heart—into the scope of the commandment. Those who harbor such anger come under the same judgment as the person who actually takes the life of another. "Raca" in v. 22 is probably the Aramaic equivalent of the Greek word translated as "fool" in the same verse. Both are used frequently as a form of insult in Rabbinic literature, and are variously translated as "empty-headed," "nit-wit," "moron," "block-head," although their actual meaning is uncertain. Like those who commit murder, those who harbor anger are also judged by both the religious (Sanhedrin) and divine ("hell of fire") authorities.

Does this, however, mean that all anger is evil in the eyes of God? The Authorized Version, which renders v. 22 with the additional "*without a cause*," adds an important element to its interpretation. This addition is considered by most scholars to be a later gloss. This is because, although it is found in most Greek manuscripts of the Gospel, it is not found in the best. Be that as it may, this gloss helps us to understand what Jesus actually meant. Not all anger is evil in the sight of God. There is such a thing as righteous anger. Jesus himself manifested righteous anger when he chased the merchants and dealers out of the courtyard of the temple (John 2:12-17). Furthermore, Jesus himself called the Pharisees "fools" in Matthew 23:17, using the same word as here. In the context of the Sermon, however, Jesus was referring to unrighteous anger, the anger of pride, hatred, and revenge. Jesus equated this kind of anger with murder, even if it does not ultimately result in physically taking the life of another.

Jesus then presents two illustrations to bring home the point that he had just made. "*If*" (v. 23) shows that they are hypothetical, and "*therefore*" establishes their connection to the preceding statements. The two illustrations are different in some important details. The first is taken from worship, the second from a law court. The first concerns a brother, the second an enemy. Both, however, have to do with reconciliation.

Verses 23-24 describe a man who was about to offer a sacrifice to God in worship. As he approaches the altar, this person suddenly remembers that his "brother has something against [him]." Interestingly, Matthew's version is different from Mark's (Mark 11:25). In Matthew the worshipper remembers that his brother has a grievance against him, while in Mark, he remembers that he has something against his brother. Whichever case it may be, reconciliation was expected; and it must be initiated by the worshipper before he brings his offering to God. John Stott has modernized this for us: "If you are in church, in the middle of a service of worship, and you suddenly remember that your brother has a grievance against you, leave church at once, and put it right. Do not wait till the service has ended. Seek out your brother and ask his forgiveness. First go, then come. First go and be reconciled with your brother, then come and offer your worship to God." Reconciliation is more urgent than the sacrifice itself. Reconciliation is more important in the eyes of God than religious rituals. Hence the sharp command: "Leave your gift." The worshipper must interrupt this solemn rite to attend to it. If he does not, then the sacrifice itself would be meaningless.

The second illustration is set in a law court and concerns an enemy (vv. 25-26). The person concerned faces legal action for an unpaid debt. He must try to settle the debt before the legal process is set in motion. Stott again: "If you have an unpaid debt, and your creditor takes you to court to get his money back, come to terms with him quickly. Make a settlement out of court. Even while you are on your way to court, pay your debt. Otherwise, once you reach the court, it will be too late. Your accuser will sue you before the judge and the judge will hand you over to the police, and you will find yourself in gaol. You will never get out till you've paid the last penny. So payment *before* prison would be much more sensible."

Both illustrations urge immediacy of action. The Christian who becomes aware that he has offended another must seek reconciliation immediately. The Matthean passage suggests that this initiative must be taken even if no offence was intended. This sense of urgency and immediacy of action emphasizes the importance of reconciliation in the Christian life. Without reconciliation it is impossible to love God and neighbor truly. Without it, even our most pious acts of worship at the altar become a sham. This passage not only urges us not to harbor unrighteous anger, it challenges us to exercise Christian love consciously by taking the initiative to mend broken or strained relationships. The passive avoidance of anger is of a piece with the active pursuit of reconciliation and peace. This spirituality goes beyond the external demands of the law and touches the horizons of grace. It brings to light the very essence of the Gospel. For is this not a reflection of divine grace, of the reconciliation made possible by Christ, because of which those who were once enemies of God can now call him "Abba, Father" (Romans 5:1-11; 8:12-17)?

Avoiding Lust (Matthew 5:27-30)

In this passage, Jesus moves from the sixth commandment to the seventh. With the same formula, "You have heard that it was said . . . But I say to you," Jesus draws out the full implications of this commandment. The Jewish rabbis had interpreted this commandment as prohibiting the act of adultery. Jesus went beneath the surface and dealt with the problem of lust. Adultery is the outward manifestation of the often hidden problem of lust. And if the outward act is to be properly understood, its inward motivations must be exposed. Thus, Jesus pressed his hearers to go behind their actions and reflect on that which compelled them to act in this way. True spirituality resides in our heart and in our attitude. And if true spiritual growth is to take place, we must probe deep into our hearts and discover our true orientation in the inner recesses of our being. This is what the Sermon on the Mount challenges us to do.

"You have heard that it was said, 'Do not commit adultery.' But I tell you that anyone who looks at the woman lustfully has already committed adultery with her in his heart" (vv. 27-28). Several important things will impress themselves upon us when we reflect on these words. First, this statement helps us to understand the act of adultery itself. By this statement Jesus impressed upon his hearers that the act of adultery is more than just physical. Adultery violates the relationship between the husband and his wife. Adultery therefore has a personal side; it is the betrayal of the marriage covenant. Furthermore, by going behind the actual act of adultery to the lust that inspires it, Jesus was asserting the fact that adultery involves more than just the physical body or the genitals. It involves the mind and the heart. And because this is so, infidelity or "adultery in the heart" can take place even before the physical consummation of adultery. Perhaps this is the fuller implication of what Jesus meant when he said to the crowd who wanted to stone the woman caught in adultery, "Let him who is without sin cast the first stone."

Second, Jesus makes a clear distinction between looking and lusting. Jesus did not by this statement prohibit his disciples from looking at a woman, but lusting after her. To lust is to burn with sexual desire. Here Jesus was referring to a state of mind, a preoccupation that inflames sexual desire. Again, Jesus was not merely referring to the physical aspects of sexual attraction. He was referring to a deliberate act of willfully desiring or imagining a sexual relationship. This is the very nature of lust. Its subtlety lies in the fact that it is so much related to human sexuality that there is a tendency for us to excuse it by saying that it is part of our make-up as sexual beings. Lust would then be treated in a supercilious and cavalier manner and its potential danger brushed aside. But, as Christian spiritual writers throughout the ages have recognized and warned, the lust that whets man's desire will willy-nilly be consummated in all forms of external sins: fornication, adultery, incest, and sodomy. Thus, when Jesus interprets this seventh commandment in this way, he includes in it all forms of sexual sin, not just adultery.

In this statement Jesus brings out yet again the depth and subtlety of sin. Sin is not only a matter of actions and deeds; it is the matter of the heart. Sin, therefore, has its roots at the very center of our beings. The outward actions are but a symptom, a manifestation of that which is deeply imbedded in human nature. The problem with the Pharisees and the teachers of the Law was that they failed to grasp this very essential nature of sin—its depth and subtlety. They were contented with the externals, with mere deeds. In so doing, they merely dealt with the symptoms and not the disease. By going behind the seventh commandment and by drawing out its full meaning, Jesus exposes the very essence of human sinfulness. The fact that we have not physically committed adultery does not mean that we are guiltless. There are many men and women who would never dream of committing the act of adultery. What about matters of the heart? What about sinning in the mind and in the imagination? This is exactly what Jesus was addressing. His statement exposes the extent of human sinfulness.

If the foregoing verses bring out the subtlety of sin, the next few emphasize its seriousness. "If your right eye causes you to sin, gouge it out and throw it away. It is better for you to lose one part of your body than for your whole body to be thrown into hell. And if your right hand causes you to sin, cut it off and throw it away. It is better for you to lose one part of your body than for your whole body to go into hell." These are severe words. How are we to understand them? Some readers may know that a theologian of the early church, Origen, took some of the sayings of Jesus literally. After reading Matthew 19:12, in which Jesus said that "some men have made themselves eunuchs for the kingdom of heaven." Origen castrated himself. Are we to follow the hermeneutics of Origen? Definitely not!

The sayings in these verses are an example of Jesus' use of dramatic figures of speech, and should therefore not be understood literally. Jesus was not advocating mutilation, but mortification. The seriousness of sin requires radical acts of self-denial and discipline. Thus, in essence, Jesus taught that we should take deliberate actions to ensure that we do not put ourselves in situations in which we will be tempted to sin. To put it very concretely, if watching certain movies or reading certain magazines causes us to sin, then "pluck out our eyes"—do not go to such movies or read such magazines. Similarly, if our hands (the things that we do) and our feet (the places that we visit) cause us to sin, then "cut them off"! Don't do them, and don't visit these places. Behave as if we have already plucked out our eyes and cut off our hands and feet. This is what mortification means. It is to take sin seriously and respond to it radically. The principle here is that we must hate sin, and we must do everything within our power, by God's grace, not to allow sin, even in its embryonic stage, to have a foothold in our lives.

In this passage, Jesus emphasizes the importance of our eternal destiny. Twice he stresses that "It is better for you to lose one part of your body than for your whole body to be thrown into hell" (5:29b, 30b). We should order our lives in a way that our final salvation is not compromised. This means that we must hate and put aside those things that are harmful to our souls. We must not allow the things of the flesh to prevent us from yielding to the Spirit. This teaching is elaborated by Paul in Romans 8. The Christian who has received the Spirit of God must live according to the Spirit and not according to the flesh. To live according to the flesh—a possibility that is open to the Christian—is death, but to live according to the Spirit is life (Romans 8:6). We must therefore not feed the flesh, or, to put it in the graphical language of Martyn Lloyd Jones: "There is a fire within you; never bring any oil anywhere near it, because if you do there will be a flame, and there will be trouble." Rather we should restrain the flesh and keep check on its appetites and lust. It is better for us to be "cripples" in this life than to lose everything in the next. "It is better for you to lose one part of your body than for your whole body to go into hell." These words teach us that we should put our salvation and eternity before everything else. For, surely, nothing could be more important to man than his eternal happiness with God!

CHAPTER THREE

Ethics of the Kingdom II

Concerning Divorce (Matthew 5:31-32)

MATTHEW 5:31-32 must be read together with Matthew 19:3-12, which records Jesus' discussion with the Pharisees about marriage and divorce. Although Matthew 19:3-12 presents a more detailed account of the teaching of Jesus, it is fundamentally of a piece with what he says here in the Sermon. Thus the question raised by the Pharisees in 19:6, "Why then did Moses command one to give a certificate of divorce, and to put her away?" (RSV), corresponds with 5:31. Both refer to the specific provision found in Deuteronomy 24:1-4. And the reply of Jesus in 19:6 corresponds almost *verbatim* with 5:32, including the formulaic "But I say to you." Both passages therefore contain Jesus' explicit teaching regarding marriage and divorce.

In 5:31 Jesus cites a regulation in the Mosaic Law (Deuteronomy 24:1-4) that allows the husband to issue a bill of divorce. But one must understand the nature and thrust of this passage in order to grasp what the Old Testament teaches about divorce. This passage does not require, recommend, or even sanction divorce. Its object is to prohibit the man to remarry his former spouse if he divorced her, for that would be "detestable in the eyes of the Lord" (v. 4). Strictly speaking, this passage does not institute or even approve of divorce, but simply treats it as a known practice.

The first three verses are all the conditional (*protasis*) part of the sentence. The consequence (*apodosis*) does not begin until v. 4. Thus, the argument that we have in this passage goes like this: *if* a man divorces his wife, and *if* he gives her a bill or certificate of divorce, and *if* she leaves and remarries, and *if* her second husband divorces her or dies, *then* her first husband may not marry her again.

To be sure, this bill in Deuteronomy was also meant to protect the woman. The bill gave her the right to marry someone else after her husband had divorced her. It is important to note that, unlike the situation of modern times, marriage was not an option for a woman in those days. Marriage provided financial security and was therefore a matter of survival for the woman. Prostitution was the only other alternative. In Jewish society and culture, divorce is always the prerogative of the husband. The wife may appeal to the court if she wishes to be divorced from her husband. And if her plea should be accepted, the court would direct the husband to divorce his wife. In Jewish society, divorce is the inalienable right of the husband.

The condition for divorce seemed clear in Deuteronomy. The husband is allowed to divorce his wife if he finds some "indecency" in her. However, by Jesus' day, what constituted "indecency" had become very problematic in Jewish culture. To be sure, it had to do fundamentally with sexual impurity. But, as the Old Testament scholar Peter Craigie has famously observed, "the statement is so succinct that all the details are no longer clear." This ambiguity opened the door to a plurality of interpretations. Soon divorce bills were issued because husbands found some physical deficiencies in their wives, or because their wives were unable to bear children. In the rabbinic school of Hillel, the range of interpretation was so broad that a husband was allowed to divorce his wife if he did not like the dinner (Mishnah *Git*. 9:10)! Great rabbis like Hillel and Shammai debated long and hard about what would justify a man to divorce his wife. But they failed to understand the binding nature of marriage and the importance of fidelity. This was precisely the emphasis that Jesus made in his antithesis to the common practice of the day.

Against the liberal attitude towards divorce that was prevalent during his day, Jesus emphasized the sanctity of the marriage covenant. Marriage is not only a lifelong commitment between a man and a woman; it is also an institution established by God, as 19:4-6 makes clear. In answering the questions of the Pharisees regarding divorce, Jesus points them to "the beginning," that is to say, to the original plan of God. He quotes almost *verbatim* from Genesis 1:27, thereby stressing the profound bond between a man and a woman that marriage establishes. Indeed, their bond to each other is stronger than even their ties to their parents. "For this reason a man will leave his father and mother and be united with his wife." Husband and wife will become "one flesh"; they will be two separate individuals who can no longer live as individuals, but must now live for each other, giving themselves freely and selflessly to one another.

From the standpoint of creation, this bond is possible because man and woman were originally of one flesh—woman was taken out of man, she was from the very beginning part of man (Genesis 2:22). But marriage is also a covenant between husband and wife. And God himself established this covenant when he brought the woman to the man in the Garden of Eden. One might say that God was the first matchmaker. God thus wills marriage as a community of love and as a life-giving community. This unity, which was instituted by God himself, is not to be broken by man: "What God has joined together, let no one separate." So sacred is this union and so serious is its violation that Jesus insists in 5:32 that if a man divorces his wife for any other reason except unchastity, he causes her to commit adultery. And if a man marries this divorced woman, he too is guilty of adultery.

Two problems present themselves. The first is the exception clause in Matthew 5:32 and 19:9, which is problematic for many exegetes because it is only found in Matthew. Both Mark and Luke excluded this clause in their accounts, thereby making Jesus' prohibition of divorce absolute. This has led some scholars to argue that Matthew had added this clause to reflect the reality that faced his own community, namely, that divorce and remarriage will continue to occur. But this position is rather speculative. It is more reasonable to argue, as some scholars have done, that Matthew simply made explicit what Mark and Luke had assumed. Thus, as David Hill pointed out, since Jewish law in the first century *required* a man to divorce his adulterous wife, it may be assumed by the other Gospels "as an understood and accepted part of any teaching on the subject of divorce." The exception clause, according to this view, belongs to the original teaching of Jesus on marriage and divorce. The second problem has to do with the meaning of *porneia* (translated in the NIV as "marital unfaithfulness"). Roman Catholic exegetes have interpreted *porneia* to mean not sexual immorality or adultery, but incestuous marriage. Hence the *New Jerusalem Bible* renders the phrase thus: "except for the case of illicit marriage." But this view is untenable simply because illicit marriage would not have been recognized as a true marriage, and therefore would not have required a divorce. Thus, it is more natural to translate *porneia* as sexual immorality or adultery.

Let me then summarize Jesus' teaching on marriage and divorce. Jesus emphasizes the permanence of the marriage covenant by grounding it in creation, and in the original intention of God. By so doing, Jesus stresses that divorce is certainly not in keeping with the divine will concerning the husband and the wife who have been united as one in holy matrimony. *Put simply, the rule is: No divorce!* This also implies no remarriage. The permission that is given in the Mosaic law for the husband to divorce his wife is, strictly speaking, not in accordance to the divine will. It is a concession that Moses had provided because of the hardness of heart among the people. Jesus recognizes the fact that this condition continues to be prevalent. Thus, although he stresses the permanence of marriage, he too allows divorce on grounds of infidelity. But, he stresses—against the prevalent practices of his day—that *it is on grounds of adultery and adultery only that divorce is allowed.* Sexual promiscuity and adultery may be said to be the de facto exception to the rule. Jesus also stressed the fact—often missed by the rabbis in their discussions on divorce—that divorce is never *commanded*, it is merely *permitted* under the above-mentioned circumstances. The implication is that adultery *does not necessitate* divorce. Whenever possible, forgiveness and reconciliation should be sought. Because of the sanctity and the permanence of marriage, divorce under the above-mentioned circumstances should always be the last resort.

Concerning Credibility (Matthew 5:33-37)

In this passage, we come to the fourth antithesis between Jesus' teaching and the common interpretation and practice of the Mosaic legislation. I must stress (yet again!) that Jesus does not in the Sermon attempt to nullify the Law. At the beginning of this major section (Matthew 5:17ff), it must be recalled, Jesus categorically and emphatically asserted that it was never his intention to abolish the law. His intention was rather to fulfill it. Thus, his authoritative and formulaic "But I say to you" is not purposed to override the Law, but to bring out its true meaning and essence. It is to penetrate beneath the letter and touch the spirit of the Mosaic legislation. It is to expose the erroneous conceptions that have

Ethics of the Kingdom II 29

emerged in the history of interpretation that resulted in the proliferation of human traditions that distort rather than capture the true intent and meaning of the Law.

"You have heard that it was said to the people long ago, 'Do not break your oath, but keep the oaths you have made to the Lord.' But I tell you, 'Do not swear at all'" (33-34a). This sounds very much like an absolute prohibition to any kind of oath-taking, and some Christians have interpreted this statement in this way. For instance, the Members of the Society of Friends, commonly known as the Quakers, have understood this statement literally as an absolute ban on all forms of oath-taking, and they have even refused to take an oath in the Court of Law. To be sure, their desire to obey God's Word is admirable. But in this instance, they have misinterpreted (and therefore misapplied) the teaching of Jesus. Jesus in this passage did not forbid the practice. He was concerned to deal rather with the abuses and the perversions that were connected to oath-taking. His teaching here is not only to emphasize the solemnity and seriousness of taking an oath, but also to go beyond, as he often does in the Sermon, to stress the integrity of the spoken word.

It must be remembered that both the Old and the New Testaments do not forbid oath-taking, even oaths that are made in the name of God. Deuteronomy 10:20 is an injunction regarding this: "You shall fear the Lord your God. Him you will serve, to him you will cleave, *and you will swear by his name.*" In fact, in the Old Testament, the oath that is made in the name of the Lord carries so much weight that it is often used to prevent litigation. This is clearly seen in Exodus 22:10-11, in which a case of adjudication between two individuals is presented. "If a man deliver unto his neighbor an ass, or an ox, or a sheep, or any beast, to keep; and it die, or be hurt, or driven away, no man seeing it: then an oath of the LORD be between them both, that he hath not put his hand unto his neighbor's goods; and the owner of it shall accept thereof, and he shall not make it good." In the New Testament, too, oaths are regularly made in the name of God. Paul, for instance, commonly swears in the name of God as he calls upon God as his witness (see Romans 1:9; 2 Corinthians 1:23; 1 Thessalonians 2:5, 10; cf. Philippians 1:8). Jesus himself may be said to have taken an oath in the name of God. In Matthew 26:63-64 we have the description of the trial of Jesus by Caiaphas. Frustrated by the fact that Jesus had remained silent throughout the interrogation, the high priest said, "I put you under oath before the living God, tell us if you are the Messiah, the Son of God." To which Jesus replied, under oath: "You have said so," or, "It is true; I confess it." Thus, Jesus himself was under oath and took an oath.

What Jesus challenges here in the Sermon was not the Mosaic Law, but Pharisaic misappropriations. The Pharisees had built up an entire legalistic system around the Old Testament teaching. For instance, there is found in the Jewish code called the Mishnah a whole tractate given over to the discussion of the questions of oaths—which oaths are more binding than the others. Sometimes the discussion borders on the ridiculous. For instance, one rabbi argued that if you swear *by* Jerusalem, you are not bound by your vow; but if you swear *toward* Jerusalem, then you are bound by your vow. These rules that pile up one on top of the other in the Mishnah have all missed the point. The law in the Old Testament on oath-taking is to ensure truthfulness. The regulations that were proliferated in the Mishnah seem to be directed at creating loopholes that allow a person to get away with deception. Put differently, the rules set up by the Pharisees and scribes lead not only to a misunderstanding of the intent of the Deuteronomic law pertaining to oath-taking, they led to its perversion. They become the basis for swearing evasively. And such swearing is but a justification for lying.

Jesus, therefore, was interested in the question of truthfulness, integrity, and credibility. If people are to play games with oaths—Jesus was in effect saying—then we should do away with oaths altogether. They no longer serve their purpose of ensuring truthfulness. Thus, in vv. 33-34, Jesus says: "But I say to you do not swear at all, either by heaven, for it is the throne of God, or by the earth, for it is his footstool, or by Jerusalem, for it is the city of the great King. And do not swear by your head, for you cannot make one hair white or black." Also in these verses Jesus relates all forms of oath-taking to God. To swear by anything is to swear by God, for God is behind everything. No oath is trivial. Jesus expands on this in Matthew 23:16-22:

> Woe to you, scribes and Pharisees, hypocrites! For you travel land and sea to win one proselyte, and when he is won, you make him twice as much a son of hell as yourselves. Woe to you, blind guides who say, "Whoever swears by the temple, it is nothing; but whoever swears by the gold of the temple, he is obliged to perform it." Fools and blind! For which is greater, the gold or the temple that sacrifices the gold? And, "Whoever swears by the altar, it is nothing; but whoever swears by the gift that is on it, he is obliged to perform it." Fools and blind! For which is greater, the gift or the altar that sacrifices the gift? Therefore he who swears by the altar, swears by it and by all things on it. He who swears by the temple, swears by it and by him who dwells in it. And he who swears by heaven, swears by the throne of God and by him who sits on it.

But more importantly, and here we get to the very heart of Jesus' teaching, what really counts is the truthfulness of our speech and the integrity of our character. As the New Testament scholar Donald Hagner has rightly remarked in his commentary on this passage: "A truthful person need not swear at all." "Let your word be 'Yes, Yes' or 'No, No.'"

Anything that is beyond the truth "comes from the evil one," whom John describes as the "father of lies" (John 8:44). The teaching of Jesus is echoed by James (James 3:5-6), who describes the tongue as a destructive evil, which is uncontrollable and which cannot be tamed, full of poison. Thus, the Christian must let his speech be without deception and duplicity—he must let his "Yes" mean yes, and his "No" mean no. As someone who claims to have the truth, the Christian should be mindful of the fact that he must always be truthful in his speech and authentic in his deeds.

Turning the Other Cheek (Matthew 5:38–42)

We come now to one of the most difficult passages in the Sermon on the Mount. "Do not resist an evil person. If someone strikes you on the right cheek, turn to him the other also." Many Christians have found the teaching of our Lord in this passage to be simply impractical, and many non-Christians have accused Christians of inconsistency because of the Christians' failure to put this injunction to practice. How are we to understand this provocative teaching of Jesus?

We begin by examining the context. Using his familiar formula, Jesus cited certain Old Testament prescriptions that were originally instituted to provide the judicial system of Israel some guidance for punishing crime. These laws had the dual purpose of defining justice and restraining revenge. They were based on the principle of exact retribution in which the punishment meted out must match the crime, and the compensation to the victim cannot exceed his loss. However prescriptive the laws might appear to be, it must be remembered that they were meant to be restrictive as well. They were meant to ensure that reprisals for injustices suffered were of the exact same kind and to the precise degree.

For example, a man whose brother was murdered could not massacre the entire family of his brother's assailant. But it must also be remembered that these laws were given to the Jewish people qua nation. They served as a guide for the judiciary and not for personal vendettas. Thus, these laws were not intended to sanction revenge. On the contrary, they were meant to ensure justice, thereby preventing the Jewish people from taking matters into their own hands.

In Jesus' day, the restrictive aspect of these laws was forgotten and the prescriptive aspect emphasized. Once this happened, the motivation was how far one might extend one's retaliation without breaking the law. Furthermore, the scribes and the Pharisees extended the applications of these laws beyond the judicial boundaries and allowed personal revenge. They had therefore totally ignored the injunction in Leviticus 19:18, "Do not seek revenge or bear a grudge against one of your people, but love your neighbor as yourself. I am the Lord." The teachers of the law had therefore completely missed the true intentions of these laws. They turned these laws on their heads, allowing the very thing that these laws were fashioned to prevent. Again, the provocative words of Jesus were aimed at bringing their hearers back to the proper intention of the Mosaic legislation.

But Jesus went beyond this. The Mosaic legislation was instituted because of the hardness of men's hearts. These laws in particular were designed to prevent revenge. But the disciples of Jesus must go beyond the letter of the law and discover the spirit of the law. His disciples must not only be concerned with asserting their rights. They must be willing to give up their rights in some circumstances for the sake of others. Jesus pointed then to the principle of love that must govern the attitudes and the actions of the disciples. Love does not seek its own good, but the good of its object. True love (*agape*) is selfless, and it is this kind of love that should characterize the spirituality of his disciples, whose righteousness must surpass that of the Pharisees.

Jesus presented four examples to illustrate this new ethic. If a man insulted a disciple of Christ by hitting him on the right cheek, the disciple should be willing to suffer another insult rather than seek recompense from the law. If a disciple was involved in a lawsuit that involved a suit of clothes, he should give his opponent his cloak as well. Though it was very unlikely that a lawsuit would be fought over clothes, the example illustrated the principle nonetheless. The disciple should gladly surrender what rightly belonged to him. The third example was taken from the Roman practice of enlisting the help of civilians. Again, the disciple in such a situation should do more than was required of him. And finally, the disciple should not turn away from those who borrow money from him. Instead he should gladly lend whatever he had.

Any reader of these verses would conclude that the teachings of Jesus are very difficult to put into practice. These verses remind us of the saintly Monseigneur Charles François-Bienvenu, the bishop in Victor Hugo's *Les Miserables*, who surely is their near perfect embodiment. We must remember that these examples serve to illustrate a principle. We must not forget the context in which these examples were presented. To repeat, Jesus was dealing with the legalistic mindset of the Pharisees and the scribes, who turned the law that was originally meant to serve the interest of justice into an avenue for personal revenge. Furthermore, Jesus pointed out to his disciples that they should be concerned with the spirit rather than just the letter of the law. God requires more from his people than their minimal adherence to the legalistic demands of this legislation. He requires them to live according to the ethic of love, in which they will be willing to even give up their rights. Thus, by these examples, Jesus was saying to his disciples: "Don't be concerned about yourselves all the time. Don't always be asking, what's in it for me?" As Christians we must be careful not to interpret these examples with the same frame of mind as the Pharisees. We must not understand them to be prescriptive in a legalistic way. We would have misunderstood the intentions of Jesus if we, for instance, said—on the basis of the third example—that we should only go the second mile, and not an inch more!

We must turn now to the statement made by Jesus in v. 39: "Do not resist an evil person." These words have been misinterpreted by some of their most illustrious readers. Tolstoy insisted that society should get rid of soldiers, policemen, and magistrates because they resisted evil. He saw the statement as the key that unlocked the rest of the New Testament. If the commands of Christ were obeyed, Tolstoy believed, people would live peaceably with one another and the Kingdom of God would be consummated. In a similar vein, Gandhi's philosophy of non-violence was inspired by these words. Gandhi accordingly advocated quiet persuasion and the willingness to endure suffering as a proper political strategy. We must reject these recommendations not just because they are idealistic, but because they are unbiblical. The New Testament clearly teaches that the state is a divine institution, and that its office-bearers are the "servants of God" who are appointed to maintain law and order and to administer justice (see Romans 13:1; 1 Peter 2:13-17). Even the presence of anti-Christian governments and totalitarian regimes (Revelation 13) should not alter this fundamental biblical truth. Jesus' teaching would be inimical to that of the rest of the New Testament if the interpretations of Tolstoy and Gandhi are correct.

Space does not allow a fuller discussion of this important topic. What must be pointed out here is that a distinction must be made between the duties and functions of the state and those of the individual. We must remind ourselves yet again of the context in which Jesus made this statement.

He was addressing the erroneous use of the law to allow personal revenge. He was urging that his disciples must disabuse themselves of the idea that they could resist evil by taking matters in their own hands. Seen in this way, Jesus' teaching does not contradict that of the rest of the New Testament. Rather, the New Testament expands on the teaching of our Lord. Thus Paul wrote to the Romans: "Do not repay evil by evil. Be careful to do what is right in the eyes of everybody . . . Do not take revenge, my friends, but leave room for God's wrath, for it is written: 'It is mine to avenge; I will repay,' says the Lord . . . do not be overcome by evil, but overcome evil with good" (Romans 12:17-21).

Loving Our Enemies (Matthew 5:43–48)

In the previous passage (Matthew 5:38-42), we encountered the difficult teaching of Jesus concerning the ethic of non-retaliation. In this passage, Jesus urges his disciples to do what may appear to most readers to be quite impossible: to love their enemies. Jesus begins, as he always does in this segment of the Sermon, by quoting from the Old Testament. "You have heard that it was said, 'Love your neighbor and hate your enemy.'" The only problem with this quotation from Leviticus 19:18 is that the latter half is not part of the original text. The latter injunction was taken by the Rabbis to be an implication of the command to love one's neighbor. This conclusion was a serious error, because it excludes one's enemies as one's neighbor, an exclusion that the Old Testament itself does not urge. In fact, the Old Testament teaches that one should not treat one's enemies differently from the way one treats one's neighbors. Thus, "if you see the donkey of someone who hates you fallen down under its load, do not leave it there; be sure you help him with it" (Exodus 23:5). And "if your enemy is hungry, give him food to eat; if he is thirsty, give him water to drink" (Proverbs 25:21). Thus, the first corrective that Jesus brought was to highlight a *non sequitur* in rabbinic teaching. The command to love one's neighbor does not allow one to hate one's enemies, for the word "neighbor" *includes* one's enemies.

This clarification brings us to the heart of Jesus' teaching in the passage, and also to the difficulty of this passage. The problem does not lie in understanding what the passage says, but what it commands the disciples of Christ to do. Is it really possible for one to love one's enemies? It may be possible for one to choose not to retaliate. It may be possible to tolerate an enemy. But is it possible to *love* him? Before we answer this question, we must clarify some other matters. The first is, Who is our enemy? For the disciples of Christ, the "enemy" is never an abstract force. The enemies of the disciples were people who hated them because of their love for the Lord. They were those who persecuted them because they saw them as revolutionaries who would disturb the peace that Rome allowed them to enjoy. They were the religious leaders and the champions of popular religion who resented Jesus. Jesus also knew who his enemies were. They were those who were hostile towards him, and those who would use whatever influence and power they had—religious or political—to stop him from teaching the people. They were those who betrayed him, those who mocked him, and those who crucified him. These were the enemies of Jesus Christ and his disciples. And it is to these people that the disciples must show Christian love.

Jesus did not simply talk about the idea of loving one's enemies. He gave a very concrete example how this love is to be expressed. "Pray for those who persecute you." The disciple of Christ who suffers persecution must overcome the hurt, the anger, and the hatred that he has for his oppressors. Instead of seeking revenge or devising ways of destroying his enemies, the disciple must learn to pray for them. Through prayer, the disciple, instead of condemning his persecutors, stands on their sides, and pleads for them to God. In prayer, the disciple does for his persecutors what they cannot do for themselves; he brings them before God and pleads on their behalf for divine forgiveness and restoration. In prayer, the disciple demonstrates the ineffable greatness of Christian love. In prayer, the disciple does not distance himself from his enemies, but stands with them and intercedes for the grace of reconciliation to be actualized in their lives. In prayer, the disciple of Christ is imitating his Lord, who in the incarnation stood among those who hate and despise him and who on the cross prays, "Father, forgive them," so that those who hung him on the tree of the cross might be reconciled to God.

The example that Jesus provided in this passage, however, was not himself, but God. The disciples are to love their enemies so that they may show themselves to be "sons of [their] Father in heaven" (5:44). Jesus appeals to divine providence as an example of the unconditional love of God. The love of the Creator becomes the model of unconditional love and the motivation for the behavior of the Christian community. God the Creator shows himself to be the God who cares and provides, and his providential love is lavishly and universally given without discrimination. "He causes his sun to rise on the evil and the good, and sends rain on the righteous and the unrighteous." Divine benevolence is directed towards all mankind, and it is this model of love, this way of loving, that the disciples of Christ are required to emulate. This passage presents to us that breathtaking truth that God alone is to be the standard of all Christian morality and that the disciples of Christ are expected to conform to this standard. They are to be "perfect as their heavenly Father is perfect," for it is this that distinguishes them from the heathens: "If you love those who love you, what reward will you get? Are not the tax collectors doing that?"

Ethics of the Kingdom II 39

Some commentators have protested that the ethical demand of Jesus in this passage is simply unrealistic. Montefiore, for instance, has argued that this demand of Jesus is simply strung so high "that it failed to produce solid and practical results just where its admirers vaunt that it differs from, and is superior to the ethical codes of the Pentateuch, the Prophets and the Rabbis." Others are even more brutal. Heine could write: "If the dear God wants to make me happy, he lets me experience the joy of seeing that on these trees about six or seven of my enemies are hanged. With a sentimental heart I will forgive them all injustice before their death . . . Yes, one must forgive one's enemies, but not before they are hanged."

In 1992, I spoke at an ordination service in North-East London. I can still remember what I said to the candidate for ordination that day: "God has called you to the ministry of reconciliation, to proclaim his love, and to preach the Gospel of healing and forgiveness to his people." I have uttered such words many times before in a variety of contexts. But on that occasion, I felt the full gravity of every word in a way I had never felt before. This is because the congregation that I was addressing that day was made up of refugees from Zaire. Every single member of that congregation can tell stories of horror, of atrocities, of cruelties, of torture, and of murder. In every face one can see the shadow of suffering, pain, and sorrow, those experiences that leave permanent scars in the deepest recesses of their beings. I ask myself, Can these people who have suffered so much at the hands of their enemies really love their enemies? What do words like "reconciliation," "healing" "forgiveness," which fly off our lips so frequently and sometimes so flippantly, mean to them? Is forgiveness and reconciliation possible?

The question can be put differently. Can the imperative to love one's enemies be understood as a "natural" demand? The answer to this question is "No," for the presuppositions behind this command are "unnatural." They point to that marvelous and unheard of entry of the kingdom of God into a sinful world. It is impossible for the natural man to obey such a command. But for the new community that will emerge as the result of the presence of the kingdom of God inaugurated by Jesus, such love has become a possibility. The dawn of the new order enables us to realize that what is "normal" in human society belongs to the order of sin. It helps us to realize that that which is deemed to be "realistic" is, in fact, determined by the distorted perceptions of a fallen humanity. But this old order will pass away. A new order will emerge, and with it a new ethic. Jesus' command makes clear that this new order is not something that will come in some distant future. Rather it has already come, although not in its fullness. And because it has already arrived, the impossible possibility of unconditional love can indeed be actualized in the lives of his disciples, even as it continues to be an ideal for which they must continue to strive to attain.

CHAPTER FOUR

On Love and Piety

Parading Piety (Matthew 6:1-4)

THE FIRST four verses of Matthew 6 set the context for the succeeding twelve, which deal with spiritual disciplines such as almsgiving, prayer, and fasting. These were common acts of piety among the Jews of Jesus' time, and, with the exception perhaps of fasting, they continue to be so in the context of the contemporary church. They are, in fact, basic expressions of piety that can be found in most religions. Expressions of piety, this passage points out, can become gauges for spirituality, and the means for parading one's religiosity for the sake of gaining public approval and praise. This is the issue that Jesus addresses here in this passage. His comments are directed at the Pharisees, although they are not specifically mentioned in this passage. John's Gospel provides an account of the Pharisees' ravenous hunger for praise. In one passage, the Pharisees are described as being more concerned with the praises of men than that from God (John 12:43), while in another they are described as pandering for each other's praises with little concern for divine approval (John 5:44). They would stop at nothing to satisfy their insatiable appetite for public approval and praise. Jesus warned his disciples to be careful not to imitate these religious leaders and not to parade their acts of righteousness before men (6:1b).

Verse 2 allows us a glimpse of the pomp and fanfare with which the Pharisees go about performing their acts of righteousness. It paints a picture of a Pharisee on his way to the synagogue to put money into a special box. He is led by a contingent of trumpeters who were supposed to alert the poor. But the real reason for the presence of the trumpeters was to direct attention to the Pharisee. It is difficult to ascertain whether the trumpets here are metaphorical or literal. But their status does not in any way change the point that Jesus was trying to make. Philanthropy that blows its own horn is deplorable. It is deplorable not because it is inferior, but because it is inauthentic and hypocritical (6:2). In the Gospels we meet several kinds of hypocrites. There are those whose outward posture portrays noble intentions, but who, in fact, are motivated by evil. Those who quizzed Jesus about the law in the pretext of wanting to learn, but who were actually looking for ways to ensnare him are examples of this type of hypocrites. Another type comprises those who are full of themselves and their sense of self-righteousness. But the kind of hypocrite that is dealt with in this passage is subtler. He has convinced himself that he really has the interest of the poor at heart, being numb to his own hunger for praise. But hypocrisy of whatever brand is in the end the same. A hypocrite is an actor; he is not authentic in what he does. His piety is not from the heart; it is not genuine. It is playacting—a performance in search of an audience, the objective of which is self-glorification.

The passage makes it quite clear that those who are so superficial as to be satisfied with the praise of men, and who are willing to do anything to get it, will receive their reward. They will indeed receive public applause, but that is all that they will get! Deuteronomy 15 teaches that God will bless those who give out of a genuine love for the poor and a genuine desire to obey God's Word. But if, like the Pharisees, one gives to earn the respect and admiration of men, to impress men and draw attention to himself, all the blessings of God will be lost. Those who do this are foolish, for they have substituted the reward from God with the reward from men. They are more interested in the tangible and the immediate, more attracted to the approval and praise of men than the approval of God. Consequently, how God looks upon their action becomes unimportant. Those who behave in this way have no regard either for others or for God. They are only concerned about themselves: they want to look good; they relish the applause. They feel good about looking good and become victims of self-deception by eventually even believing that their benevolence is genuine.

The disciple of Christ must not do likewise. Instead, when he gives, he must ensure that his left hand is ignorant of the deeds of his right. He must give in secret. With this overwhelming metaphor, Jesus taught that giving must be private. Two points must immediately be made in anticipation of possible misunderstandings. First, Jesus is not saying that secrecy is itself meritorious. Second, this statement must not be read through lenses tinted by modern individualism. Jesus is not advocating the privatization of religion. The context has to do with the ostentatious display of piety, and not the comparison between public worship and private devotion. Privacy has the virtue of ensuring that one's giving is truly motivated by love, and not, even in part, prompted by public applause. Privacy ensures that no one will know when and what we have given. Even our left hand does not know what the right hand has given! No one, that is, except God. He knows. And he knows not only that we have given, but that we have given with the right attitude and motivation because we have done so in secret. And he will reward us.

The church must seriously ask herself if she is sometimes also guilty of the ostentation that Jesus here condemns, not only in her deeds of charity, but also in her other "acts of righteousness." There is much attention given to the social dimension of the Gospel in evangelical churches in recent times. This, of course, is to be welcomed, and, for us Methodists, it is the recovery of one of the most powerful features of our tradition. But we must be careful that our sometimes flamboyant and loud overtures to the community, especially in the light of recent trends of community service in the churches in Singapore, do not degenerate into nothing but ostentatious displays of piety devoid of substance, depth, and truth. The culture that the church imbibes can sometimes make her insensitive to this danger. Ours is a culture in which it is not enough for one to do good. One must be *seen* to be doing so. Publicity is key. Also in this culture, image is more important than reality. Our culture mirrors remarkably the Pharisaism about which this passage warns. The hypocrisy of the Pharisees has to do with that which appears to be rather than that which really is. Hypocrisy exerts itself to conjure images in order to impress. The Pharisees are their own spin-doctors—they adorn themselves with phylacteries and with their long fringes; they wear pious looks, and claim the best seats in the synagogues. They do everything to ensure the desired *effect*. But they are whitewashed tombstones, beautiful on the outside, but on the inside are full of dead man's bones. The teaching of Jesus here is clear: Do not be like them! The disciple of Christ must not live in contradiction where his outward appearances do not jibe with who he really is. The disciple of Christ must be authentic in being and act.

On Prayer and Performance (Matthew 6:5-8)

In this passage, Jesus provides another example of religious exhibitionism, this time, in connection with the practice of prayer. In ancient Judaism is to be found a widely practiced routine of daily prayer in which the recitation of the

Eighteen Benedictions were made obligatory three times a day, morning, noon, and evening. Prayers were to be made facing the direction of the holy of holies of the temple in Jerusalem. The practice of praying in synagogues and also at street corners was quite widespread, as was the practice of praying while standing. It was common practice for temple trumpeters to blow their instruments during the daily afternoon sacrifices at the temple as a signal that prayer should be offered. A Jew would then stand right where he was in the street corner, turn towards the temple, and offer his prayer. This fact alone militates against the view that Jesus was concerned with externalities, and that he wanted to abolish certain practices. Jesus was concerned here with inner motives, and not with external acts.

"When you pray, do not be like the hypocrites" (6:5). Here, the hypocrisy concerns the activity of prayer, the most common, and yet the most profound of religious activities. Prayer is communion between finitude and infinity, between creature and Creator, between man and God, a communion that is made possible only because of the privilege that has been accorded to man by God. And yet, even this most sacred act is infected by the gangrene of sin and pride. Hypocrisy is an affront to true religion. The Pharisees prayed not because they loved to pray or they loved the God they were praying to. They prayed because they wanted the recognition, endorsement, and admiration of the public. They stood in synagogues or at street corners with arms raised towards heaven, praying aloud. But at the same time, they would steal quick glances to see if people were watching. In their hypocrisy, the Pharisees were using religion for their own selfish ends, to promote themselves so that the people's esteem of them would be elevated.

Religious pharisaism is alive and well in our churches today, and much introspection is needed to discover its often subtle manifestations. The person who leads in public prayer; the energetic worship leader; the enthusiastic Bible study group leader; the charismatic pastor—everyone is susceptible to it. But the problem with religious pharisaism is not just its subtlety but also its perversity. It corrupts a religious act by emptying it of real content. It replaces truth with falsehood, piety with pride, God with self, even as it performs these acts with practiced precision, sophistication, and intensity. It is deceptive, because it gives lip service to God while drawing attention to the worshipper. The ultimate objective of religious pharisaism is to satisfy the insatiable hunger of one's ego for recognition, adoration, respect, praises.

After exposing the hypocrisy of the Pharisees, Jesus turned to his disciples and told them what he expected of them. And here we find some of the most profound statements on prayer: "But when you pray, go into your room, close the door and pray to your Father, who is in unseen," Again, in contrast to the public display of piety by the Pharisees, Jesus emphasized secrecy or privacy. Jesus was not abolishing public prayer or worship. The early German pietists took this counsel literally and prevented any audible prayers in the worship service. But this was surely a misreading of this passage. Jesus was not concerned about valuing private prayers over public ones. He was addressing the ostentatious display of piety. He was not designating the private chamber as the only appropriate place for prayer. Rather, his object was to illustrate the proper attitude to and in prayer.

There is, therefore, no special virtue in praying in one's chambers, no special virtue in secrecy or privacy. Such acts, too, can serve as means of drawing attention to oneself, as Chrysostom, the fourth-century church father, was quick to alert his hearers. It is possible for one to go into one's chambers to pray only after telling others about it! Bonhoeffer even went so far as to say that secrecy and privacy could not really deter an ego hungry for an audience. That ego could be its own spectator! "I can lay on a very nice show for myself even in the privacy of my own room" (Bonhoeffer). It is not so much the place where one prays, but the attitude in which one comes before God's presence that is the emphasis here. True prayer is directed to God; it is the communion between the creature and his Creator. True prayer should not be showcased.

There is another characterization of religious pharisaism in prayer that Jesus addressed. Jesus told his disciples that when they prayed, they should not, like pagans, keep babbling, thinking that by their profuse speech they stood a better chance of being heard. Pagan prayers can be said to be techniques that, if meticulously applied, would produce the desired results. One such technique practiced by pagans is the exhaustive and relentless naming the gods. The more names on one's list, the more one's chances are of having one's requests granted. Another technique is repetition. It is believed that the more repetitious the petition, the greater the chances of it being granted. Yet another technique is eloquence, in which the person who prays will heap phrase upon eloquent phrase to ensure a hearing. In contemporary Christianity, too, prayer is sometimes regarded as not much more than a technique.

Jesus warns his disciples against this. Prayer is fellowship with God. It is communion with God, the one who is omnipotent and omniscient—all-powerful, all knowing. There is no need for eloquence or repetition. Sincerity and transparency are far more important. But it does appear that v. 8 can even be stretched to imply that in the end, there is no need for prayer! "[F]or your Father knows what you need before you ask him." The context, however, rescues theology from abstraction and from arriving at wrong conclusions. Jesus is not saying by this that there is no need to pray. He is clarifying what prayer really is. Prayer is not about manipulating God to answer our request. God cannot be manipulated; he is all-powerful. God is all knowing. So God cannot be tricked into granting what we want. In fact, he knows our needs much better than we do. Prayer, in the final analysis, is about fellowship. It is the privilege that God extends to his rational creature made in his image to converse with him, to enjoy his company, and to be totally dependent on him. This would surely help us to see the ugliness and depravity of religious pharisaism. It violates the relationship between God and man. But this statement helps us to see the true nature of prayer is to be found in the covenantal relationship between God and his people. And it is with this understanding that we are furnished with the necessary background for our reflection on what has been commonly called "The Lord's Prayer."

Hidden Spirituality (Matthew 6:16-18)

It has become almost axiomatic in our modern work culture that one should not only be working hard, but *must be seen to be doing so*. To labor quietly and unnoticed is sheer folly to the modern sensibility. Some would even go so far as to say that to be seen to be industrious is far more important than to be actually industrious. This mindset, when brought into the religious sphere, will result in the kind of piety that Jesus is addressing here. Thematically, the passage that we are now considering is of a piece with the first eight verses of chapter six. The Lord's Prayer in vv. 9-13 is an excursus that interrupts the otherwise seamless message in 6:1-18. Jesus is here dealing with spiritual showmanship and advocates a hidden spirituality for his disciples.

The particular practice that is discussed in this passage is fasting. Fasting was a common practice in the time of Jesus. In the Jewish religion, two kinds of fast were observed. The public fasts were observed during special feast days, like the Day of Atonement, while individual or private fasts were observed in relation to some important occasions. The Jews fasted when undergoing distress or in times of deep penitence. The most frequently mentioned example is perhaps David's distress over the illness of the child conceived by Bathsheba in an illicit affair (2 Samuel 12:13-14). Public fasts were often conducted in the time of national tragedy. For example, the nation of Israel fasted after the death of Saul and Jonathan (1 Samuel 31:13; 2 Samuel 1:12). Public fasts were also conducted in connection with the supplication of the nation for divine favor and mercy before a war or after a calamity (Judges 20:26; 1 Samuel 14:24; 2 Chronicles 20:3). Individual and group fasts were for a variety of purposes, especially the confession of sin and the cultivation of self-humiliation before God (e.g., Nehemiah 9:1-2; Psalms 35:13; Isaiah 58:3), or the making of supplications to God (Exodus 24:18; 2 Sam 1:12; Ezra 8:21-3). The Pharisees in Jesus' time fasted twice a week, on Tuesdays and Thursdays. These fasts were voluntary in nature, and sometimes served as wonderful opportunities for spiritual showmanship.

It must be said at the outset that Jesus did not put a ban on fasting. "When you fast . . ." indicates, rather, that he expects his disciples to fast. Fasting has been an important spiritual discipline throughout the history of the church. In the early church, the religious act of fasting was commonly associated with solemn prayer, and with the setting apart of leaders of the church (Acts 13:2-3; 14:23). From the second century onwards, fasting is seen as an important religious activity. An early document, the *Didache*, states that just as the Jews fast twice a week, so must Christians. The document suggests Wednesdays and Fridays, instead of Tuesdays and Thursdays, as days of fast for Christians. We may conclude from this that it was normal for Christians in the early church to fast at least once a week. John Wesley tried to revive the teaching of the *Didache* and encouraged Christians to fast twice a week. In fact, he was so serious about fasting that he refused to ordain anyone who did not fast twice a week. The benefits of fasting are numerous. Fasting and prayer enable us to develop habits of self-denial and self-discipline. Fasting enables us to have control over our appetites. It enables us to identify ourselves with the poor and disenfranchised. Fasting opens our eyes to issues of justice, and compels us towards righteousness (Isaiah 58).

Jesus did not object to fasting but condemned the ostentation in fasting. "When you fast, do not look somber like the hypocrites do . . ." The Greek word that is translated as "somber" in the NIV can also be translated as "sullen" or "gloomy." The Pharisees, when they fasted, deliberately looked sullen and gloomy to show people that they were engaged in this religious act, and that they were holy men. That they went out of their way to make themselves conspicuous is made perfectly clear in the second half of v. 16: "for they disfigure their faces to show men they are fasting." Thus, they walked around with faces contorted with gloom, parading their piety and inviting public approval, applause, and respect. They were hypocrites because everything they did—their religiosity—and indeed their very lives was a lie. There was no correspondence whatsoever between their private lives and the public image they projected. They wanted to be *seen* as holy and righteous men. But, in fact, the outward display only served as a camouflage for their wickedness. Thus they deserved Jesus' stinging condemnation: "Woe to you, teachers of the law and Pharisees, you hypocrites! You are like whitewashed tombs, which look beautiful on the outside but on the inside are full of dead men's bones and everything unclean. In the same way, on the outside you appear to people as righteous but on the inside you are full of hypocrisy and wickedness" (Matthew 23:27-28).

This—"inside and outside"—is the first set of antitheses that Jesus used to expose hypocrisy. The second set of

On Love and Piety 51

antitheses is "secret and public." To his disciples Jesus said: "When you fast. Put oil on your head and wash your face, so that it would not be obvious to men that you are fasting." Put differently, Jesus was exhorting his disciples not to make a public display of their religiosity. Again, I must caution against a modernist reading of this passage. Jesus is not saying that worship or religious acts like fasting do not have a communal and corporate dimension. Jesus was not advocating a private religion, in the modern sense. The emphasis here is against hypocritical ostentation. The exhortation is towards authenticity. The Pharisees who wanted the praise of men would have received their reward in this regard (v. 16). They would enjoy the accolades that the public confers. But they would forfeit the reward that comes from heaven.

Christians are not immune from the lust for publicity and approval. The pastor who puts his congregation under the spell of his oration, the bishop who goes around with the air of pomp and grandeur, the worship leader who dazzles with charisma, the lay leader who prays with such awe-inspiring zeal and energy—all are susceptible to the Pharisaic spirituality, a hollow and vacuous religiosity, whose supreme goal is self-promotion. The same may be said of those who go to a religious meeting, say, a prayer meeting, not so much to pray, but to be *seen*. They make it a point to appear at certain occasions so that they may be seen and so that they may score points. They will indeed receive what they so desperately wanted—praises from men—but nothing else besides. The true disciples of Jesus, on the other hand, whose spirituality is genuine and from the heart, will receive divine approval. For God looks not at the exterior; he looks into the heart. God does not take notice of extravagant public displays of piety, but the secret intentions and motivations of the heart. And he who sees behind every false façade, whose eyes are able to penetrate every mask, will reward accordingly.

CHAPTER FIVE

The Lord's Prayer I

Our Father Who Art in Heaven (Matthew 6:9a)

WE TURN now to the prayer that Jesus taught his disciples, which is commonly called "The Lord's Prayer." In Matthew, this prayer is set within the context of the Sermon on the Mount, while in Luke it is set in a more general context of Jesus' teachings on prayer (Luke 11:1-13). Furthermore, in Matthew this prayer is set forth as a model to be followed ("this is how you should pray"), while Luke gives the impression that one should repeat the actual words of the prayer ("When you pray, say"). The structure and pattern of the prayer follows quite closely the Jewish Qaddish prayer of the synagogue, although its theology is somewhat different.

It is important for us to note at the very outset that this prayer is taught by Jesus Christ. It is through the incarnate Word that we come to know who God is, and how we should approach him. Thus, this prayer, like the rest of the Sermon, cannot be understood from any other standpoint apart from Christ. Like the rest of the Sermon, this prayer can only be properly understood christologically. In many liturgies, including that of the Methodist Church, the Lord's Prayer is said during the eucharistic celebration. The celebrant invites the congregation to join him in this prayer by words such as these: "As our Savior has commanded and taught us, so we are bold to say . . ." The invitation—worded in this way—is found in the best liturgies. This invitation reminds us that we, by ourselves, do not have the right to pray this prayer. We boldly say the words of the prayer because we are commanded to do so. And this command must be understood as grace, for because of it we now have the privilege of doing the inconceivable—approaching God and calling him "Father."

Jesus teaches his disciples to address God as "Father." Although this way of addressing God is not alien to the Old Testament, it is extremely rare. In the Old Testament, God is called Father only fourteen times. This is always done in the context of salvation history. Thus, although Israel understands the fatherhood of God as depicting the fact that he is the originator of all that there is, it is in the context of covenant, not creation, that this way of addressing God is most frequently found. To call God "Father," then, is to remember the Exodus event, in which God liberates his people and calls them his children. It points to the salvation of Israel, and the peculiar way in which the all-powerful God has covenanted his love to Israel. This address, therefore, gives Israel her identity. When Jesus taught his disciples to call God "Father," he was suggesting that, with his coming, a new Exodus was about to take place. With his coming, the people of God would be free at last. The fatherhood of God helped Israel to find strength in times of political oppression by looking back to the Exodus and by assuring herself that the God she worships is faithful and will deliver her from captivity and oppression. With Jesus, the fatherhood of God helps God's people to look forward to the day when they shall be truly and forever free. This new age has already dawned with the coming of the Son of God. And so, to call God "Father" is already to express that eschatological hope that the day of full deliverance is near.

Jesus uses the Aramaic *Abba* in this prayer. This word suggests intimacy. But let us be clear that this is neither an invitation nor an excuse to adopt an attitude of sloppy fraternizing with God. Intimacy is not synonymous with irreverence. The God whom we call Father is the "Father Almighty, Creator of Heaven and Earth," as the Creed reminds us. "Father" gives us a glimpse into the faithfulness of God, who condescends to be our covenant-partner. This means that the fatherhood of God cannot be understood in light of patriarchal and authoritarian concepts. In fact, the fatherhood of God is a challenge to such human conceptions of fatherhood, whether they receive life from socio-cultural norms and practices or from psycho-religious predilections.

The fatherhood of God must be understood in the light of scriptural revelation. In the New Testament, the fatherhood of God is portrayed supremely in the story of the prodigal son, or, if one wishes to look at the story differently, the waiting Father. Here, the father, against all expectations of law, custom, and social convention, allowed his son freedom to choose, even if this choice is misconceived. When the son returns totally devastated and humiliated, the father does not reprimand him or require him to earn his keep as a servant. Rather the first action of the father is that he runs to meet the son. This action is unthinkable in a patriarchal mode! The father runs to his son, embraces him, welcomes him, and celebrates his homecoming. Surely, this portrayal of the fatherhood of God challenges all authoritarian and patriarchal models of fatherhood.

It is in the light of this that the mystery of prayer is to be understood. Prayer is conversation between a child and his heavenly Father, who is almighty yet loving. Because God is Father *Almighty*, he knows our every need even before we utter them. He knows us better that we know ourselves. He knows our past, our present, and our future. Prayer can never be an irreverent demand for this or for that. It can never be manipulative arm-twisting. Only the fool would think that he could twist the arm of the Almighty. Because God is *Father*, prayer is always first and foremost a relationship. It can never be reduced to a technique or a business proposition, for this is not the way in which a child relates to his father. Prayer is a trusting relationship in which the child entrusts everything, indeed his very life, to the care of his Father. The true prayer of faith is one that humbly accepts God's answer as the best, even when this answer is inimical to the request. True prayer, as we shall have occasion to reflect more deeply later, is always motivated by the desire to see God's will (not ours) be done.

Addressing God as "Father," however, is not just comfortable or reassuring. It is also a challenge. Like everything else in the Sermon on the Mount, the Lord's Prayer yields many precious lessons on discipleship. To call God "Father" is to pledge our obedience to him. The supreme example of obedience is found in our Lord Jesus Christ, and the most intense moment in which this struggle of obedience is evidenced is in the Garden of Gethsemane. In those dark moments Jesus struggled with obedience: Must I do this? Can not this cup pass from me? Is there no other way? Finally, Jesus yielded fully to his Father: "Not my will, but thine be done!" When we address God as "Father," we too must live our lives in obedience. We too must say, "Not my will, but thine!" This is the way of the obedient child of God. This is the way of the disciple of Christ, whose life is an imitation of that of his Master. This is the way of the church universal, in which this prayer is prayed in solidarity and unity, transcending traditions, confessions, and denominations.

Hallowed Be Thy Name (Matthew 6:9b)

"Hallowed be thy Name" is the first petition in the Lord's Prayer. Moderns generally find it difficult to understand the gravity of the petition for two reasons. First, the name to moderns is a device that is used merely for personal designation. Apart from that, very little is made of a name. This is very different from the way in which the name was regarded in antiquity, as we shall later see. Second, moderns live in a generally secularized culture. This is true even in the context of Asia, where traditional religions seem to flourish. Post-Christian Europe is but one manifestation of secularism and cannot be paradigmatic of the way it impacts other cultures. Secularism has either demystified the sacred or confined it to the private sphere. The demands of this petition, that God's name be hallowed in every sphere of human existence, have become inconceivable to the modern mind and are thus met with resistance. Modern Christians too must re-orientate their thinking to the spirit of this petition; for we too may have imbibed too much of our culture, which obfuscates the meaning of this petition.

Scripture makes it quite clear that there is more to a name than just personal designation. A name carries with it the mystery of unique personality, and thus describes and even defines its bearer. The most intimate expression of the relationship between God and man is found in the assertion that God knows us by our names. God does not know humankind in the abstract, but individuals in their uniqueness and complexities. The name individuates us from the masses. Scripture applies this view of the importance of the name supremely to God. In the first place, Scripture tells us that God indeed has a name, and that he has revealed his name to us! In his encounter with God through the miracle of the burning bush, Moses asked: "If I come to the Israelites and say to them, 'The God of your ancestors has sent me to you,' and they ask me, 'What is his name?' what shall I say to them?" God replied: "Thus you shall say to the Israelites, 'I AM has sent you'" (Exodus 3). God is the great "I AM." He is defined by no other than himself, because there is none greater than he. Thus he is "I AM who I AM" or "I will be what I will be." God has preferred to reveal his name. He has preferred not to be a nameless God. He rejects anonymity and discloses his name, thereby putting his signature, so to speak, on everything he does.

That the name of God is profoundly related to who he is is the essence of divine revelation. God does not come as a masquerade; he does not use an alias. He comes to us as he is, and he beckons us to call him by name. Furthermore, by giving us his name, God reveals that he is a personal God. He is not some force or power. He is a personal God who tells us his name and who knows us by name. Prayer is therefore possible; it is the intimate engagement between two persons—the believer and God. Prayer is not a soliloquy, but a dialogue, and this is made possible because our dialogue partner has disclosed to us his name. But because the name of God is tied to who he is, when we pray that God's name be hallowed we are asking that God himself be hallowed. The name of God is holy because God is holy. Scripture is replete with statements about the holiness of God. Perhaps the cry of the seraphim in Isaiah 6:3 encapsulates for us the essence of the scriptural declaration of the holiness of God: "Holy, Holy, Holy, LORD God of hosts." This marvelous chorus, which thrice declares the holiness of God, identifies holiness to be the incomprehensible ground of his being. Put differently, holiness is what makes God God.

It must be emphasized here that "Hallowed be Thy Name" petitions that God make his name holy. It is a petition that God should glorify himself, for the glory of God is made manifest by his holiness. The petition, made in the passive voice, at once recognizes that God alone can make his name holy. This petition therefore prevents Christians and the Church from ever thinking that they have the power to sanctify God's name. Thus, this petition, when uttered with theological integrity, helps the church to be humble before God. It prevents the pride, so common in the church today, that leads her to think that she can vindicate God by her actions. When made with religious seriousness and with theological integrity, this petition becomes instead a call to repentance. It becomes a reminder that the church has fallen short of the standards of holiness that are set by the holy God whom she serves. As a call to repentance, this petition therefore rightly precedes a later petition in which the church prays: "Forgive us our sins." For the church that prays "Hallowed be thy Name" has all too often failed to be holy and to respond with disdain to those who would desecrate the name of God. As the German theologian Helmut Thielicke has so starkly expressed it: "The truth is that we cannot pray the Lord's Prayer to the glory of God unless at the same time we pray it *against ourselves*. And he who has not yet learned to pray this prayer *de profundis*, out of the depths of repentance, has not really prayed it at all."

But "Hallowed be Thy Name" can only be uttered by those who have experienced the unheard of grace of God. From the time when it was first revealed to Moses, the name of God has always been a name that liberates and delivers those who are held as captives, those who bear the mark of another name. God does not only reveal his name, but, in doing so, he has by his grace delivered us from slavery so that now we can be called by his name. Thus, the name of God does not only enable us to know who he is; it also enables us to establish our own identity. The name of God helps us to understand who we are, and to whom we belong. Here again, the christological dimension of this prayer cannot be marginalized. It is through Jesus Christ our Savior that we learn to pray "Hallowed be Thy Name." It is through him that we *can* pray in this way, just as it is through him that we can call God "Father." This petition is made possible by the grace of God, for it is divine grace that has made those who were once "not a people" into God's people.

This petition is therefore also a call to discipleship (for the Lord's Prayer is in actuality also the Disciple's Prayer!). It is instructive to note that this prayer contains no petition for self-improvement or sanctification. The prayer does not say "Consecrate *me* and make *me* holy," but "Hallowed be *Thy* Name." This, of course, does not mean that it is illegitimate to pray for God to sanctify us and make us holy. But the Lord's Prayer directs our attention to the fact that it is God who makes us holy, and in the end it is his holiness that should occupy our minds. The Lord's Prayer puts everything in its proper place. The Christian life is not ultimately about our own exertions and the preoccupation with our own progress. The disciple of Christ does not set himself up as his own goal. The essence of Christian discipleship, and, therefore, that of Christian spirituality, has to do with our willingness and desire to honor God and to allow him to work in us by his Spirit. This petition calls to question the way in which spirituality and spiritual formation have been reduced to techniques and programs (a kind of DIY spirituality) in the contemporary church. It exposes the fact that so much of the modern discourse about spirituality is generally egocentric. "Hallowed be Thy Name"—this should be the sole desire of the Christian. But this petition does not only address the inner life. It also deals with perspectives and with loyalties. Throughout her history, the Church has from time to time acted in the name of progress, science, patriotism, a denomination, and the like. This petition summons the church to examine her loyalties critically, for the Name of God relativizes all other names. "Hallowed be Thy Name" is therefore a prayer for God to be God in the Church and in the world. It says implicitly what a later petition—"thy kingdom come, thy will be done"—will say more explicitly.

Thy Kingdom Come (Matthew 6:10)

The next petition is expressed in the pregnant phrase "Thy kingdom come." In vogue today, especially in some Christian literature, is the use of the noun "kingdom" as a form of adjective. We read about "kingdom lifestyle" and talk about "kingdom principles." Such usage, however, sometimes distracts us from what Scripture does or does not say about the kingdom of God. The true meaning of the kingdom of God, its theological meaning, must be recovered in order for us to appreciate the depth and implications of this great petition. In Scripture, the "Kingdom of God" always refers to the reign and the authority of God. In the New Testament, the kingdom of God is depicted christologically. Jesus Christ, the Son of God, has been given all authority to exercise this rule. He will do so, according to 1 Corinthians 15:24-28; and when he does, all of God's enemies, those anti-God forces that are hostile to the lordship of God, will be put under his feet. The book of Revelation similarly tells us that these hostile forces will eventually be defeated, and the kingdoms of this world will become the kingdom of our Lord and of Christ who shall reign forever (11:15). The kingdom of God is portrayed as the redemptive rule of God as well as an eschatological reality.

The petition is for God's kingdom to come. With the coming of the messiah, the kingdom of God has already become a reality in our world, although its presence in human history remains a mystery, and its fullness is yet to be. The petition for the kingdom of God to come therefore has to do with the future presence of the kingdom, its consummation, at which time every knee will bow and every tongue confess the lordship of Christ. The petition therefore signals the fact that the kingdom is already here—already there are to be found among human beings the heirs of Christ, citizens of the kingdom—and the fact that it is not yet here in all its fullness. In other words, the petition "Thy kingdom come" helps us to understand the time in which we live. It helps us to understand time; it helps us to understand our time. For by this petition, we have come to the realization that the future already impinges upon the present; that time cannot be understood as a series of events without purpose or direction. By this petition we come to the realization that time, our time, must be defined by the future coming of the kingdom of God.

When we pray "Thy kingdom come," we are, in fact, praying for God's time to come. This prayer comes against the creed of the Darwinian view of the world. "Thy kingdom come" is not a prayer for the prolongation of time, typified by the Darwinian quest for survival. "Thy kingdom come" is a prayer for the true fulfillment of time to come. Needless to say, this way of announcing time makes our time controversial. The clock is not the true measure of time. The true measure of time is, according to this petition, determined by hope. The petition forces us to ask fundamental questions about our time, questions that push us to reflect deeply upon our present existence in time. Is our time empty, hopeless, and void of the future? Or is our time vivified by hope and filled to the brim with the future?

Something must be said about the coming of the kingdom at this juncture. The kingdom about which we are concerned, it must be remembered, is the kingdom of *God*. This petition reminds us of the fact that only God can bring about his kingdom. This emphasis must be made against tendencies found in both liberal and evangelical Christianity. In liberal Christianity, the kingdom of God is totally existentialized and secularized. The kingdom of God no longer refers to that wondrous penetration of time by eternity. The kingdom of God, in liberalism, is the domestication of eternity by time. God's kingdom becomes the onward march of human culture, a march that is determined by an evolutionary view of culture. In some evangelical circles, the same force is at work, albeit more subtly. The coming of the kingdom is tied almost absolutely to the church and her various endeavors. The coming of the kingdom is dependent on how hard the church works towards the evangelization of the world, and how concerted her missionary programs are.

This prayer reminds us that the kingdom about which we pray is *God's* kingdom. Its coming will depend on God's schedule, not ours. By this, we are, of course, not implying that the church should be passive. The church must try her utmost to bring the Gospel of grace and love to the world. But there is a difference between obedience and presumption. The church acts out of presumption if she thinks that the coming of the kingdom is tied to her program and efforts. Both passivity and presumption are attitudes of disobedience. Both the passive church and the presumptuous church have yet to understand the meaning of the petition "Thy kingdom come." For in this prayer, the pilgrim church acknowledges the fact that her hope should be based solely on God and not on her programs and efforts. In this prayer, the pilgrim church acknowledges that her duty is to fulfill God's agenda, not her own.

In this way, this petition can only be made in faith. In it the pilgrim church acknowledges her total dependence on God. But there is another sense in which this prayer is a prayer of faith. "Thy kingdom come" must mean that the world as it is could not yet be characterized by righteousness, joy, and peace. The evidences of the kingdom are sometimes seen and experienced. But they are often faint and fleeting. To pray this prayer requires faith, because this prayer invites scorn from the world. The world cannot understand this prayer, for it can neither see the mystery of the kingdom of God nor identify with the hope that energizes this petition. The world sees this prayer as yet another form of escapism, as fantasizing about some future utopia that will only dissipate in the face of the harsh realities. So many such utopias have come and gone. Euphoria has turned to disillusionment. Hope has turned to despair. Is "Thy kingdom come" just another one of those utopian dreams that will soon fizzle away to nothingness as the twenty-first century plods on?

This is only true when the Lord's Prayer has become nothing but one of those religious niceties that one has become accustomed to since one's association with the church. It is true when the Lord's Prayer is seen merely as the articulation of a religious idea or an expression of religious aspiration. But this is not what the Sermon on the Mount and the Lord's Prayer are about. We started with Christology, and if we are to make sense of this petition in the Lord's Prayer, we must return to Christology, if only to remind ourselves that our hope is based on what Christ has accomplished. In our eucharistic rite, we often declare "Christ has died, Christ is risen, Christ will come again." This declaration has profound theological implications to our discussion. "Christ has died, and is risen" points to the past—to the first coming, death, and resurrection of the Messiah. "Christ will come again" points to the future, to his coming as Judge, and with it to the closing of the age. Our faith in the future is rooted in history. To put it even more accurately, our faith in the future is rooted in those events of greatest density in history—the death and resurrection of Christ for our salvation. Because God has done this, he will surely also fulfill his promise in bringing his reign upon all humankind. Christians live in the light of this hope. We live in the light of the kingdom of God that, one day, will come in all its fullness. It is thus fitting that "Thy will be done, on earth as it is in heaven" is prayed in almost the same breath as "Thy kingdom come." Put differently, the coming of God's kingdom in the future has ethical implications for the present. The petition "Thy kingdom come" does not inject passivity into the Christian life. Rather, it makes the Christian aware of the pressing demands of the ethics of the kingdom in his or her life. "Thy kingdom come," prayed by the disciple, should remind him or her of the demands of discipleship.

CHAPTER SIX

The Lord's Prayer II

Our Daily Bread (Matthew 6:11)

THIS PETITION, which appears right in the middle of the prayer, may seem odd to some. The prayer has thus far been concerned with lofty matters regarding God's Name and Will. This petition, which has to do with "our daily bread," at first glance appears rather mundane and trivial by comparison to earlier concerns. But closer study and deeper reflection not only will show this first impression to be mistaken, it will also open our eyes to many a wonderful insight regarding God and regarding ourselves. This petition brings us to the threshold of this prayer, and this is indicated by the pronouns. Thus far, the prayer has been concerned with God: *thy* name, *thy* kingdom, *thy* will. But now there is a shift in emphasis to man: *our* bread, *our* debts, *our* temptation, *our* struggle with evil. But the shift should not cause us to think that there is a break in the prayer, or that there is now a change of theme. The prayer is a unity, and its theme—the relationship between God and man—remains the same throughout. Even when the prayer directs its attention to human need, it is still concerned with the glory of God. In the same way, also, one may say that every aspect of this prayer has to do with human need.

The first thing that this petition teaches us is that we should learn to appreciate the "little things," the ordinary and the mundane. We should never take them for granted, not only because we need them, and we cannot live without them, but also because they are gifts from God. They are the gifts of grace. While it is true that man should not live on bread alone, this petition reminds us that man cannot live *without* bread either. It takes but a little effort in reflection (an effort that we do not make often enough) to realize that these "little things" actually take a very high priority in our lives. Simple things like nourishment and rest are indispensable to human life. Their absence or lack would cause us to look at life itself very differently. Those who enjoy the rapturous beauty of the music of Rachmaninov or the aesthetic brilliance of the art of van Gogh or Da Vinci often fail to consider how very differently we would respond to these splendid works of art if we were hungry or shivering in the cold. To put it plainly and brutally, if we were starving, we would gladly trade a Monet for a loaf of bread! The little things, the things that we take for granted, the so-called trivia, play a very important role in our lives. "Give us today our daily bread" reminds us of the importance of these "little things," and teaches us never to take them for granted.

The Bible, to be sure, speaks against "materialism"—the philosophy and outlook that idolizes material possessions and wealth. But the Bible teaches a "holy materialism"—a theology that helps us to see that matter is God's creation and that the material needs of man are important. This simple petition for daily bread speaks of this in a profound way. On the one hand, this petition warns us against looking at bread and our full stomachs as ends in themselves. That is materialism. But on the other hand, this petition transfigures the status of "trivialities" and gives "little things" like bread a special dignity because they are gifts from God. They are evidences of divine grace. This prayer teaches that the Christian must never idolize bread. But he must not despise it either. The Christian must recognize that his daily bread comes from God. He is to receive that which God has given to him with thanksgiving and gratitude. This petition also warns us against the hypocrisy that pretends to be above such "little things," the hypocrisy that pretends to be preoccupied only with the "big things," with "spiritual" matters. This petition exposes hypocrisy of those Christians who behave as though the affairs of this life do not affect them. Such heavenly-mindedness may be very impressive, but it is not the requirement of the Gospel. In fact, such heavenly-mindedness may in the end be just a form of pride, a pride that blinds us from seeing the greatness of the God who is interested in the "little things."

This petition shows that God and bread belong together. This is true whether the movement is from God to bread or from bread to God. The significance of this truth cannot be under estimated. The Bible does not present a rigid dualism; it does not present a compartmentalization of reality into the sacred and the secular. Bread and God cannot be separated. Therefore, bread cannot refer to mere economics, for there is no such thing as mere economics. Put differently, the Christian cannot think of bread only in terms of itself. Bread, for the Christian, must be understood theologically. Only when we see bread in this way will we recognize the fact that this petition is also at the same time a call to repentance and conversion. For if bread is inseparable from God, then our attitude towards it will impinge upon our attitude towards God as well. This petition transforms the way we see even the commonest things, because we are here reminded that they belong to God and come from God. When this happens, then even the commonest thing becomes a revelation of the Word of God. Bread becomes the revelation of the grace and providence of God. The theologian Gerhard Ebeling is therefore right to say that "the ultimate aim of the prayer for our daily bread is not that we should receive bread as such, but that we receive it for what it is—as God's bread, in which and with which is God's word."

But what may this petition mean in an affluent society like ours, where the daily bread is taken for granted? What may this prayer mean for a consumerist society that is constantly spoiled for choices? What may this petition mean for a society that always grasps for more? To be sure, this petition reminds us that all that we have and enjoy comes from God and that we should never take that for granted. But this petition also encourages us to rediscover the meaning of the word "enough." It encourages us to be contented with what we have and to keep our acquisitive impulses in check. "Give us today our daily bread" teaches us that there is really no such thing as private property. Everything, including something as basic as bread, belongs to God. This prayer tells us that bread is made available because of God grace. It therefore teaches us to be dependent on God, and to recognize his providential love. This recognition must cause us to repent of all sense of self-sufficiency and pride.

This petition for daily bread should also sensitize us to the plight of the oppressed and the hungry. "Give us today our daily bread" must be prayed with the willingness to share our "bread with the hungry" (Isaiah 58:7), for this is true religion. This petition, therefore, should open our eyes to issues pertaining to justice. It should awaken us to the fact that God wishes to minister to the whole person, and the church must do the same. The prayer depicts humanity as hungry and needy. It drives home the point that the material needs of human beings should never be under estimated. The church, consequently, must not substitute the care of the body for the care of the soul. The entire person, both body and soul, must receive attention. Above all, this prayer brings us back to basics and urges us towards contentment and simplicity. It is when we recognize that we are dependent upon God for the most basic things—food, shelter, even the air that we breathe—that this prayer will issue in doxology, the petition will become thanksgiving and praise.

Forgive Us Our Sins (Matthew 6:12a)

With this petition we come to the very heart of the Gospel. The message of the Gospel is the message of divine forgiveness and reconciliation. This petition cannot be made without reference to Christ, because without him and his atoning work on the Cross, there can be no forgiveness. Once again, we are reminded of the centrality of Christ, not only in this prayer, but also in the entire Sermon. The basis of divine forgiveness is the atoning and reconciling death of Jesus Christ. In the same way, the basis of the Christian life, portrayed here in the Sermon on the Mount, is the finished work of Christ. Those who pray this petition must have experienced the reality of the gracious and forgiving God in Jesus Christ. Those who are able call God "Father" know that they can also pray with confidence "Forgive us our sins." For God our Father is the God who forgives; he is the Father who waits eagerly for the return of his child. And when he sees his child, he will run to him, embrace him, and welcome him home. This petition reveals the heart of God.

Like the previous petition, this petition also reveals a human need. It reveals the fact that we are sinful, that we tend to be rebellious, and that we are not always mindful of the grace of God. We belong to a culture in which sin is no longer in our vocabulary. We have found so many ways to explain away sin, so many ways to fabricate excuses. Under the influence of psychology, sin is no longer theologically defined, even by our theologians and Christian pastors. Sin has been psychologized; its solution no longer lies in redemption but in therapy. Similarly, in this so-called Age of Biology, the concept of sin has all but disappeared, as has the concept of morality. Some geneticists have maintained that human behavior is genetically determined. If this is true, then freedom has become an illusion and morality has become irrelevant. The concept of sin is made redundant through the medicalization of social problems and the genetification of behavioral traits. This petition urges us away from such reductionistic accounts and points us to the fact that the human condition is more complex and requires a *theological* explanation.

The relationship between bread and sin, established in this petition, should not be overlooked. The little conjunction "and" establishes this relationship. The relationship brings out a very important insight on what it means to be human. Human beings need both bread for the stomach and forgiveness for the soul. Without bread, human beings will die; but there is another kind of death that will take place when man goes without the grace of divine forgiveness. There is a sense in which we are more attuned to our physical needs. The stomach, it has been said, grumbles when it is in need of food. We take notice of this and attend to it almost immediately. But the soul has a softer voice—and this already soft voice is often drowned by the barrage of loud voices that come from our insatiable culture. These voices direct us to a trillion things that we "need." But it neglects the one thing we do need: forgiveness. The voice of the soul often goes unheard. But it must not go unheard! I have said earlier that man cannot live *without* bread. Now the emphasis must be made on the fact that man *cannot live by bread alone*. He is to live by the Word of God. And the most precious word that comes from the lips of God is forgiveness.

But what does forgiveness mean? Forgiveness does not mean that our evil deeds are undone. What was done remains done; it cannot be undone. Forgiveness does not mean that God does not regard our sins seriously. The romantic idea of forgiveness and magnanimity cannot be used to develop a theology of forgiveness. Scripture presents divine forgiveness as issuing out of the sacrificial death of Christ on the Cross.

The powerful symbol of the Cross banishes all sentimental notions of forgiveness and reconciliation. Forgiveness means that in the eyes of God, we are no longer sinners. Because of divine forgiveness, we are able to say, from the profoundest depth of our conscience, that we are no longer guilty. To be forgiven by God is to be liberated from the sin and guilt that torment and imprison us. The story of the paralytic presents a powerful picture of what it means to receive divine forgiveness. When Jesus told the paralytic that his sins were forgiven and to get up and walk, the physical healing helps us to understand the spiritual transformation. Sin paralyses. Just as at the word of healing the paralytic breaks free from his physical paralysis, so also by the word of forgiveness he is set free from the spiritual paralysis brought about by sin.

The context in which sin is mentioned in this prayer is important. The Lord's Prayer speaks of sin in the context of forgiveness. This means that divine forgiveness is greater than the greatest sin. Man is assured of God's forgiveness if only he can overcome his superficiality and cowardice and receive the Word of Truth and liberation from God. The context in which sin is mentioned warns us of two dangers, both of which are the strategies of the accuser. First, the accuser often succeeds in showing us the immensity of our sin and obscuring the greatness of divine forgiveness. As a result, we become faint-hearted, unsure of our own status before God. We fail to accept forgiveness; we fail to enjoy it and live by it. Many Christians today are paralyzed by this deception. They wonder how God could ever forgive them, since they cannot forgive themselves for what they have done in the past. They become miserable and handicapped. This petition emphasizes that forgiveness is indeed available because of what Christ has accomplished on the Cross. Second, the accuser often misleads Christians into taking an unhealthy and inordinate interest in the sins of others. Instead of forgiving others, these Christians become engrossed by the sins of others and spend time either in gossip or in criticism. This petition emphasizes the priority of forgiveness in the Christian life.

Just as we have received forgiveness, we are to forgive others as well. The Christian who has truly experienced the grace of divine forgiveness must know how important it is and be willing in turn to forgive others. Thus, this petition calls for personal and social responses. The divine forgiveness that we have received must set us in motion toward others. This insight is not new. In fact, it has already been discussed in the Sermon. Jesus told his disciples that if they were offering their gift and suddenly remembered some unresolved conflict, they were to leave their offering, and be reconciled with the person(s) concerned (5:23-24). Later in the Sermon Jesus will present the same instruction differently. He tells his disciples that they cannot expect God to forgive them if they do not forgive others (6:14-15). The divine forgiveness that we receive from God must spur us to forgive others, thereby enabling them to experience the liberation that forgiveness can bring. The prayer for forgiveness becomes an instruction in discipleship. Forgiveness, Jan Mili Lochman reminds us, "is not a one-dimensional matter, a one way street."

And Lead Us Not Into Temptation (Matthew 6:13)

This petition, which comes immediately after the petition for forgiveness, reminds us that we live in a dangerous world. Not only do we need divine forgiveness, we also need divine protection. This life—that is, life in our fallen world (and there is no other world but this one)—presents us with situations that can trip us up and ruin us. But when the Bible speaks of temptations, it refers to something even more sinister. It refers to the enticements that have as their goal to lead us away from God. Temptations—*all tempta-*

tions—are intended to tear us away from God and lead us towards false gods. The universality of temptations is recognized by all theologians and spiritual writers. Luther expresses this with great clarity and forcefulness: "We are beset before and behind by temptations and cannot throw them off." Luther goes on to say that there are two situations in which temptations threaten us. First, temptations threaten in situations of weakness. Sickness, poverty, dishonor, rejection—all these make us vulnerable to temptation. They incite us to anger, hatred, bitterness, and impatience. As a result, we either harden our hearts against God or we resign ourselves to them and refuse to take responsibility for our lives. Second, temptations threaten in situations of strength. Those who are in privileged positions, and who are doing well in life are, according to Luther, susceptible to temptations of licentiousness, debauchery, arrogance, avarice, and vainglory. This petition is therefore for everyone. Those who think that they have no need to pray this way have already succumbed, perhaps unwittingly, to the sin of arrogance and self-sufficiency.

The Christian has three enemies. The first enemy is from within. Temptations begin in our own hearts because we are fallen and sinful. Scripture calls this the "flesh." We perceive the world and conduct our lives according to the dictates of our selfish ego. We grasp at that which brings us pleasure and gratification. We are hedonists and narcissists, concerned primarily with our own pleasure and advancement. This is the carnality of our "flesh," our current mode of existence in this fallen world. Our next enemy is our so-called environment. The Bible calls this the "world." Temptations that come this way are very subtle, because they are camouflaged underneath layers of custom and tradition. They are found in every country and in every culture. They influence the way we perceive ourselves and others; they even shape our attitudes towards life itself. In the context of affluent societies, shaped by materialism and consumerism, the temptation to exaggerate the value of material things and to treat them as the be all and end all of life, indeed, as that which defines life and gives it meaning, is very great. The injunction to renew our minds and not to conform to the ways of the world (Rom 12:1-2) deals directly with this. If the first enemy comes from within and the second from without—from the environment—the third enemy of the Christian comes from below—from the abyss. Scripture calls him "adversary," "accuser," "devil." At the center of the scriptural accounts of temptation we find Satan. He was there at the Garden of Eden enticing the first couple to doubt and disobey God. He was the driving force behind the torments of Job. He was there at the start of the ministry of Jesus, tempting him in the wilderness; and he was also there towards the end of Jesus' ministry, when he tried to dissuade Jesus from embracing the cross. Like a roaring lion, the devil, scripture tells us, prowls around, seeking someone to devour.

Satan's strategy is clearly revealed in the Gospel account of the temptations of Jesus in the wilderness (Matthew 4:1-11). Satan attacks Jesus on three fronts. His first attack was on the body of Jesus—his physical need. After fasting for forty days in the desert, Jesus was physically weak. Satan said to Jesus: 'If you are the Son of God, command these stones to become loaves of bread' (Matthew 4:3). This temptation amounts to this: should Jesus use his messianic powers for his own gain and to avoid difficulties and suffering? Yielding to this temptation would result in disobedience to the will of his Father. In the second temptation, Satan twists scripture in order to tempt Jesus to put God to the test. Jesus rebutted Satan by stressing that this form of manipulative bribery—demanding miraculous protection as proof of God's care—was wrong, and specifically prohibited by Scripture. In the final temptation, Satan goes for the jugular. He promised Jesus earthly power and dominion if Jesus would bow down and worship him. Jesus had to make a choice. He may either make a pact with the devil or continue to commit himself to the commission that is given to him by God. Jesus chose the latter. His response was direct and unwavering: "Get away from me, Satan." Jesus stood on the Word of God and chose, in the face of testing, to obey the will of God. The Christian must do the same in the face of difficulties and trials. "Lead us not into temptation" is the prayer of those who wish to be totally obedient to the will of God, which is the true measure of authentic discipleship.

This petition and its trailer—"Deliver us from evil"— help to provide a corrective to some of the emphases that come from the now popular Spiritual Warfare Movement. Space does not allow a thorough examination of the tenets of this movement, but only that which is immediately relevant to our present discussion—"warfare prayer." "Warfare prayer," in the parlance of those who advocate what has been called strategic-level spiritual warfare, is an aggressive challenge that is directed against demons. The name of the "controlling demon" is discovered, either through prayer or research or both; and this information is used in a prayer of rebuke against that demon. Sometimes the language of "binding" the forces of evil, and "loosing" divine blessings is used. Spiritual warfare is won, according to this theory, by correct information and technique. In other words, success in spiritual warfare is dependent on human effort, on the Christian's ingenuity and bravado (mistakenly described as "faith"). Prayer is given a new definition—for in "warfare prayer," it is the demons, not God, who are addressed.

But this understanding of spiritual warfare and prayer is totally alien to the teachings of scripture. The two petitions, "Lead us not into temptation, but deliver us from evil," point us to an entirely different direction. In the eyes of the advocates of "warfare prayer," such petitions are perhaps considered to be an act of cowardice. These petitions, however, teach us that God alone is our protector and deliverer. Without him we can do nothing. These petitions acknowledge the sovereignty of God, and our total dependence on him in the face of temptation and evil. Christian prayer is not the triumphalistic shouting of slogans or commands. Christian prayer has to do with the humble approach of a sinner to the God who loves, forgives, and protects. Faith is not willful optimism. Faith is humble trust in God. Victory over the forces of darkness does not come with the employment of certain techniques or strategies in prayer. Victory comes when the child of God takes refuge in the loving arms of his Father in heaven. This is what this petition is really about.

Deliver Us from Evil (Matthew 6:13b)

The final petition of the Lord's Prayer is profoundly related to the previous one: "Lead us not into temptation, *but* deliver us from evil." The two petitions, it may be argued, give expression to the same reality. But the latter petition says more than the previous petition and so complements it. The literal translation of the petition is tricky, and theologians and Bible scholars have debated on its intended meaning for centuries. Literally translated, the petition reads: "Deliver us from *the evil*." The presence of the definite article sparked the debate, for it can refer either to evil in the general sense, i.e., evil as an abstract impersonal force manifesting itself in certain events, or it can refer, in a personalized sense, to the Evil One, the Devil. Furthermore "the evil" (*tou ponerou*) may be either masculine or neuter, thus making both interpretations possible. Theologians, both ancient and modern, are divided. The early Greek Fathers from Origen to Gregory of Nyssa to Maximus the Confessor have interpreted "evil" here as the Devil, while the Latins from Augustine have preferred to champion the more neuter sense. Protestant theologians, with the exception of Calvin, have generally followed the Latins. Calvin insisted (rightly) that it makes little difference whether we understand evil as the devil or sin. The petition is a request for deliverance from both.

The reality of evil in the world is undeniable. Philosophers and theologians alike have been exercised over the question of the origin of evil and the co-existence of the good God and evil. If God is both good and sovereign, some reason, he would eradicate evil from this world. But because evil continues to pervade the world, God is either good but not sovereign (that is, he wishes to eradicate evil but cannot), or he is sovereign but not good (he can eradicate evil but chooses not to do so). The presence of evil, these philosophers conclude, has made the thesis that God is good *and* sovereign untenable. Scripture does not provide answers to such questions. Scripture deals with the problem of evil very differently. It does not deny the reality of evil, but points to God, who in Christ has already won the victory over evil, and who will eradicate evil in the end. This is what this petition teaches.

The petition recognizes the reality of evil and presents it as that which opposes the will of God. It acknowledges the radical nature of evil in our human situation and its omnipresence in our world. Evil is not devalued, downplayed, or marginalized in Scripture. It is presented as the dominant problem. Evil is the anti-God force that seeks to destroy the very fabric of God's creation and corrupt those who are made in his image. Thus, evil is not an occasional lapse, but a pervasive reality in the world. The history of human civilization can therefore also be read as the history of human atrocities. Evil should not be isolated to some horrific events in human history. It is not my intention to trivialize these events.

My visit to Auschwitz in 2002 has impressed upon me in a profound way the extent of human evil. I have read several accounts of the Holocaust, the most powerful being

Sir Martin Gilbert's (powerful because of its brutal honesty). But the impact of the visit was tremendous. For it was pacing through the empty barracks, the courtyards of torture and execution, and the infamous gas chamber (the frivolity of the ubiquitous souvenir shops notwithstanding) that I felt most profoundly the sadness and misery of man. But behind this sadness is the evil. The petition of course includes Auschwitz when it speaks of evil. But the petition speaks of more than this. It points to the universality of evil—to the evil that resides in us; the evil that motivates our thoughts and our actions. For evil has influenced all of us: "None is righteous, no, not one; no one understands, no one seeks for God. All have turned aside, together they have gone wrong; no one does good, not even one" (Romans 3:10-12). And evil comes from the depths of our beings: "The heart is deceitful above all things and desperately corrupt" (Jeremiah 17:9). "For out of the heart comes evil thoughts, murder, adultery, fornication, theft, false witness, slander" (Matthew 15:19). Put differently, evil is not just out there, in others. Evil is in us. This petition checks all self-righteous dissociation with evil. Evil is not only found in the compounds of Auschwitz and Birkenau. Evil is found in our shopping malls and living rooms. Evil lurks in the quiet corridors of our churches and seminaries.

This petition points us to the solution to the problem of evil. "Deliver us from evil" unequivocally makes the point that it is God alone who can eradicate evil. Evil, and its inspirer the Devil, cannot be conquered by education, social reforms, and humanitarian programs. This, of course, does not mean that such efforts must be frowned upon. The Christian church has always understood that it is her duty to expose evil, corruption, and injustice and to alleviate human sufferings. But the Christian church has also understood that, in the end, she must look to God for deliverance. Theological sobriety alerts us to the fact that evil is so deeply rooted in our world that we can do nothing to eradicate it. This petition maintains that there is another who is our refuge and help. He alone has the power to destroy evil.

With this petition, Scripture comes against a dualism that postulates the eternal struggle between good and evil. This petition tells us that the power of evil is great. But the power of God is greater. It tells that that evil is real; but the victory of Jesus over evil is also real and powerful. Prayer for deliverance must therefore be set within the context of Good Friday and Easter. This prayer cannot be understood otherwise, for it is in the Cross of Christ that this petition was answered. The petition must be understood eschatologically: it is about the ultimate deliverance from all evil. But we do not pray merely for future victory and deliverance. Our prayer is firmly rooted in the victory that Christ has already won on the Cross. It is on the basis of this finished act that we dare pray "Deliver us from evil," for only on the basis of the finished work of Christ on Calvary can we dare to hope for deliverance.

We cannot pray this prayer at a distance, for we too live in an evil world, a world of pain and suffering. In praying this prayer, we are also reminded that we are called by God to walk in obedience; and obedience brings pain and suffering—obedience opens our eyes to the evil that is before us, around us, and sometimes in us. For to obey God is to wage war against evil. As Christians, we follow our Lord in his agony in Gethsemane and in his lonely and painful ascent to Golgotha. In surrendering our lives to obedience, we become Gethsemane-people and Calvary-people. Our daily prayer for deliverance testifies to our daily struggle with evil. But in this struggle, we learn not to lean onto our own understanding and our own abilities. In this struggle, all kinds of triumphalisms are avoided. (For triumphalism is actually cowardice in disguise—a form of escapism that deliberately trivializes evil). As is true of every single petition in this profound prayer, only faith can spur us to say "Deliver us from evil." Faith is trusting surrender to the sovereign God. Faith gives us the courage to walk ahead into the darkness, and faith leads us to discover that God is there in the darkness—the world of pain and suffering. And the God who is with us in history's dark moments will deliver us.

CHAPTER SEVEN

On Seeking First the Kingdom

Money Matters Matter (6:19-24)

IN THIS segment of the Sermon on the Mount, Jesus deals with the Christian's attitude towards wealth. The stern warning with which he begins puts the relationship between Christians and material wealth into proper perspective. "Do not store up for yourselves treasures on earth, where moth and rust destroy, and where thieves break in and steal" (6:19). Store up, instead, treasures in heaven. How are we to understand this injunction? Are we to conclude by it that Jesus is essentially opposing the acquisition and accumulation of wealth and property? Is Jesus advocating a form of asceticism? If this is indeed the case—and some have concluded thus—how can this statement be applied to Christians in modern society? A close study of this passage will yield the answer to these questions.

The main thrust of vv. 19-21 is to be found in its final sentence: "for where your treasure is, there will your heart be also." In Jewish thought during Jesus' time, the heart was the center of the human body. Here, however, "heart" is used metaphorically, to refer to the center of the person's inner being, the seat of his personality. Understood in this way, Jesus is referring here to ultimate concerns. If a person's ultimate concern is material wealth, then everything he does will be directed to its acquisition and accumulation. This will be his chief goal in life, and every one of his pursuits, including his religion, will be made to serve this goal. His consummate love for material wealth will blind him to the more important things of life, and finally enslave him. Such an obsession can only lead him away from the faith. Hence Paul: "For the love of money is a root of all kinds of evil. Some people eager for money, have wandered from the faith and pierced themselves with many griefs" (1 Timothy 6:10).

Verses 19-20 teach that "Earthly wealth does not provide true and lasting security." But this statement, too, must be understood in its proper perspective. To be sure, material wealth does provide *some* security. It enables a person to enjoy the fruits of his labor, and perhaps also the fine things in life. Wealth itself must be seen as a gift from God. As we have seen in our earlier discussion on the petition for our daily bread, the Bible speaks of a kind of holy materialism. The Christian is no Gnostic who thinks that spirit alone is good and matter evil. Material wealth, and the security that it provides, are important, and, seen from a proper perspective, they are a testament of God's providential grace.

Scriptural teaching with regard to this is unequivocally clear. Material wealth must be seen as an aspect of God's providence, of which the Christian must be a good steward. The Bible speaks in no uncertain terms, for instance, about the responsibility of Christians to provide for their relatives and immediate family. Those who fail in this duty are perceived to be worse than unbelievers: "If anyone does not provide for his relatives, and especially for his immediate family, he has denied the faith and is worse than an unbeliever" (1 Timothy 5:8). Scripture also encourages the accumulation of wealth for provision for the future (Proverbs 6:6-8). This is an aspect of the stewardship over what God has provided for us. Thus, when Jesus asserts that the accumulation of earthly wealth does not provide true security, he was referring again to ultimate concerns. And when Jesus told his disciples not to store up treasures of earth, he was not objecting to their being provident—for making provisions for the future—but to their being covetous—possessing an insatiable desire to acquire more wealth. Jesus was not addressing wealth *per se*, but the way in which an unhealthy obsession with wealth can distort one's values and one's perception of reality.

Verses 22-23 bring this out more forcefully. The eye in these verses must be understood metaphorically, not literally. The "diseased" eye refers to what Near Eastern cultures often call the "evil eye," an eye that is covetous of that which belongs to another, a greedy and avaricious eye. The person with such an eye constantly lusts for wealth, and devotes all his energies to its acquisition and accumulation. He is constantly distressed by those who are wealthier than he, and spends all his time feeding his insatiable hunger for more. He is never satisfied, and the word contentment has no place in his vocabulary. The symmetrical structure of these verses suggests that the "good" eye is the opposite of the evil eye. The good eye is a generous eye, not attracted to wealth, but is ever willing to part with it. But the description here can also be taken to mean "single-mindedness." The good eye is singularly focused on God, and is likewise devoted to his purpose. The eye, therefore, in this passage is a synonym of the heart. Just as the heart—the center of one's personality—reveals the ultimate concerns of an individual, so the eye—the light of the whole body—reveals his moral condition.

Jesus' emphasis in v. 24 is crystal clear. The issue here is one of loyalties. Where should the Christian's loyalties lie—in God or in money? To be sure, this verse rules out the third possibility—that the Christian can be loyal to both at the same time. According to Jesus, this is simply impossible, for "either he will hate the one and love the other, or he will be devoted to the one and despise the other." In other words, the third route would only lead one back to the first set of choices. It is not possible to serve both God and money. In the context of this passage, Jesus is actually making the point that, for the disciple, the choice is clear. He must give to God alone his undivided loyalty and absolute commitment. The disciple who displays divided loyalty is, in fact, not demonstrating his partial commitment to God, but rather a deep-seated idolatry. Either God is served with single-hearted commitment, or he is not served at all. If God is not the disciple's ultimate concern, then something else—in this context, money—must be.

It would be wrong to think that this passage is directed only to the wealthy. The suggestion, often made in some circles, that, since the wealthy are faced with a greater temptation to make money, their idol must be challenged. Both the rich and the poor can be seduced by money and controlled by greed, grasping at material wealth in such a way that their yearning for it becomes disproportionate. Through their inordinate desire for money and possessions, both can turn these neutral objects into false gods. To ask, "How much money should a Christian keep? How much should he give away?" is also to misunderstand the intention of this passage. Jesus was concerned with one's attitude towards one's goods rather than the amount. Money and possessions are problematic only insofar as they threaten the correct spiritual attitudes that Christians are required to achieve. In a materialistic and consumerist society like ours, the danger of idolising material wealth and possessions should not be underestimated. Money has become a cultural symbol of status and power, the measure of one's worth and importance. Within this cultural ethos, money is more than just a medium or vehicle of exchange. It is a powerful, seductive force that yearns to be absolutized. The Christian can only escape its entrapment if he is single-minded in his devotion to God. Only when he is firmly focused on God and his purpose will the Christian come to the realisation that the security that material wealth provides pales into insignificance when compared to the security that heaven provides.

Seeking the Kingdom (Matthew 6:25-34)

This passage from the Sermon on the Mount will surely attract our attention in this present climate of economic gloom. "Don't worry about your life!" "Don't be anxious about food or clothes, that is, about daily essentials." In times of plenty, most of us could give our assent to such assurances without much effort. But is it still possible to do so in times such as these, when some of us have lost our jobs, while others face the prospect of retrenchment? How can we not be anxious when our businesses face the prospect of collapse in this lackluster economy? In such times, do such assurances suddenly seem vacuous and naïve? Do they seem like the ingredients of escapism, a notional cocoon for those who simply refuse to face up to reality? Would such assurances appear to be contrived, superficial, and even patronizing and insensitive?

The place to begin is to try to understand what Jesus is, and is not, saying in this passage. Perhaps we should begin with the latter, which will shed light on the former. First, Jesus is *not* teaching that we should not place value on material things. I have argued previously, when commenting on the petition for daily bread in the Lord's Prayer, that the Bible teaches what I call a holy materialism. Food, clothing, money, property—the most basic of our material needs—are all very important. Even in this passage, we are told that they are gifts from God. Thus, the Bible—and certainly this passage—does not advocate a false asceticism. We are not to think that material things are unimportant and, therefore, must be rejected. The Christian doctrine of creation tells us that God has created the material world and declared that it is good. Even the discipline of fasting, which for centuries has been so integral to the devotional life of the Church, does not contradict this profound insight. The denial of something as basic as food in Christian fasting is to remind us not to take this important provision of God for granted.

Second, Jesus is *not* advocating that Christians should not work, waiting passively for God's provision. This is the unfortunate conclusion of some who read vv. 26 and 28. It should be pointed out that birds do not simply wait for God to drop food into their beaks! Here the emphasis is not that disciples need not work, but that they need not fret. The Christian faith has produced a most profound work ethic based on concepts of responsibility, accountability, and stewardship. The Christian is a co-worker with God and is entrusted with the responsibility to care, not only for his family, but also for God's creation. The Christian faith, therefore, presents work as an integral part of God's purpose for man, something that God has foreordained. Work, it must be stressed, is not the result of sin (as some might tend to think!). Sin introduced a perversion to work, making it a burden instead of a blessing and robbing it of its value. In the experience of grace, work has been given new value and made more worthwhile. It is therefore a mistake to think that Jesus is here saying that his disciples need not work.

But what *is* Jesus teaching? The fundamental thrust of the teaching of this passage is that, while material things are important, human existence is more than just a matter of food and clothing. Needless to say, the fundamental truth, so simple and yet so profound, applies to every Christian—rich and poor—and in every circumstance of life—in plenty and in want. Human existence is impossible without basics like food, shelter, and clothing; but human existence cannot and should not be reduced to just material needs. Once that happens, the holy materialism that the Bible teaches becomes perverted into a secular materialism in which God "disappears" and Money usurps the divine throne. Now, of course, I am speaking metaphorically here. God does not

On Seeking First the Kingdom 87

literally disappear when we ostracize him from our minds. He continues to be God, regardless of our attitude towards him. Still, this metaphorical disappearance is tantamount to a *real* disappearance; for as an English proverb has put it so elegantly, what the mental eye does not see, the heart doesn't grieve for. And when that happens, when a secular materialism creeps in and pollutes the human psyche (and indeed the psyche of entire cultures!), then anything that threatens our material wealth and wellbeing becomes grievous and fatal. When existence is defined by material wellbeing, any threat against it is not only a threat to our sense of security but our very existence.

It is this form of anxiety that Jesus was referring to in this passage. Such anxieties would threaten to distract Christian discipleship and, in the end, make authentic Christian discipleship impossible. It is this anxiety that causes many a Christian, many a follower of Jesus Christ, to be sidetracked, and even to abandon the path that leads to Life. Such anxieties occupy the minds of unbelievers, as v. 32 makes clear. One may perhaps excuse them for being so preoccupied, since they do not know God. But there is no excuse for the disciple, who knows God the Creator and Provider and who has seen his providential love to his creation—to the birds and the lilies. There is no excuse for the disciple, who knows that the love of God for him is exceedingly greater than his love for other creatures. There is no excuse for the irrationality of the one who, having experienced such love, now embraces the creed of secular materialism.

But if there is *more* to existence than material wellbeing, what is this "more"? This passage describes it as "the kingdom of God and the righteousness of God." The disciple of Christ should set his mind on loftier matters—on God's kingdom, that is, his rule, and on God's righteousness, that is, his righteous commands. These should be the motivation of the disciple. He should seek them before everything, even his material comfort, and give them priority. When he does this, his perspective, his entire outlook on life (and on material wealth in particular) will change. It is not that material well-being is now suddenly no longer important to him. It still is. He must still pray "Give us today our daily bread." But he will learn the proper order. He will learn to pray "Thy will be done, on earth as it is in heaven" *before* praying for his daily bread. This is not a chronological priority, but a theological one. For the disciple, concern for the will of God must be before and above all things. When this is the case, the disciple will have mastery over his circumstances, and he can truly trust in God even though his other securities are threatened. Such mastery would allow him to say No to economic gain and wealth if their acquisition involved compromising the way of the kingdom of God. (Space does not allow further expansion on this point; but I cannot overemphasize just how critical it is for this insight to be understood as the basis of all Christian ethics!) The disciple who seeks first God's kingdom and righteousness understands the importance of material things, but will never be enslaved by them. He will never define the meaning of his existence by them. Such a disciple is truly a servant of God. And because he is truly God's servant, he is truly free!

On Judging Others (Matthew 7:1-6)

We come now to an often quoted but little understood teaching of Jesus concerning judging others. The misinterpretation of this teaching has compelled many a Christian to refrain from being critical—even when criticism is warranted and constructive—and to frown on those who are. These Christians, most of whom are sincere, fail to see the inconsistencies inherent in their own attitude. For is not their objection to the behavior of their fellow Christians itself based on judgment, which, according to their interpretation of this passage, should be scrupulously avoided? Furthermore, if their interpretation is correct, more problems present themselves. For inconsistencies are not only found in their behavior, but in our Lord's as well. In v. 6, Jesus himself goes on to speak of some people as "dogs" and "pigs," and in vv. 15-20 he warns his disciples about false prophets. All this presupposes some form of judging. Jesus made it very clear, especially in John 7:24, that judging is not only appropriate for the disciple, but also that it is mandatory. This is stressed in v. 6, as we shall see.

First, let us attend to the meaning of v. 1. If judging in this statement does not refer to making a critical assessment on the basis of legitimate criteria, and if this passage does not prohibit the disciple from making all forms of judgments, what does judging refer to here? The context, particularly vv. 3-5, helps us to answer this question. These three verses describe a person who is able to see very clearly the speck in the eye of his brother, but who fails to see the log in his own eye. The contrast between the speck and the log is significant. The speck refers to anything that can get into someone's eye. It is not improbable that Jesus had sawdust in mind. Speck is of course used metaphorically to refer to some slight or insignificant shortcoming. Log, however, suggests the exact opposite. Jesus uses exaggerations—even to the extent of being ludicrous (!)—to bring his point across. A speck is placed next to a log, an inconsequential fault alongside a huge failure. The irony is obvious: the person whose faults are outrageously blatant fails to see his own failure but is quick to notice the insignificant shortcoming of his brother.

Through the use of this colorful hyperbole Jesus brings out the meaning of his earlier statement found in v. 1. The word "judgment," which is ambiguous in both Greek and English, is now clarified. It should be clear that Jesus was not referring to all types of judgment in his prohibition in v. 1, but only judgment of this sort—that of a censorious, self-righteous, and hypocritical individual. Such a person is capable of the most damning and unfair judgment. He condemns others because he thinks that he is morally and spiritually superior to them. His egoism has blinded him, and he is unable to see his own failings and the uncharitable nature of his attitude. His pride has made him a deluded, self-serving man, who thinks himself to be infallible.

It is pertinent to note that even in these verses Jesus does not question the correctness of his observation or the necessity of correcting the shortcomings of the other person. It may very well be the case that this man has judged correctly, and that his brother does need to attend to his shortcoming. But so long as he does not get rid of the log in his own eye, so long as he does not attend to his own failings, he has no right to judge and condemn his brother. Verse 6 complements v. 5. Jesus is here advocating humility. When a person, in meekness and prayerful self-criticism, removes the log from his own eye, he can, and, in fact, must help his brother to remove the speck from his eye. Accordingly, the judgmental person will come under the judgment of God (7:2). Thus, the censorious person, who is unforgiving and without love, has, by his own arrogance, shut himself from the forgiveness of God.

Verse 6 is problematic, and some commentators cannot see how it fits in this passage. Some early exegetes interpreted this verse as referring to the exclusion of unbelievers from the Eucharist, since "what is sacred" is sometimes interpreted as "holy food." Thus in *Didache* 9:5, we read: "Let none eat and drink of your Eucharist except those who have been baptized in the name of the Lord. It was concerning this that the Lord said, 'Do not give dogs what is holy.'" But this is hardly the purpose of this saying. Others have interpreted it in line with the preceding verses. Thus, according to this interpretation, "dogs" and "pigs" here refer to those who have been told about their shortcomings but who refuse

On Seeking First the Kingdom

to deal with them. But this interpretation appears forced and contrived. So is the interpretation that says that this verse is a sort of directive against evangelizing Gentiles. "Dogs" and "pigs," Calvin rightly insists, cannot refer to the Gentiles!

This verse, to be sure, is related to the preceding verses, but in a different way. It is intended to warn disciples of the converse danger, namely, the failure to be discerning. Thus, v. 6 not only brings in the balance; it also prevents the preceding verses from misinterpretation. The "pigs" in this passage are not only unclean—they are wild and savage. Similarly, "dogs" does not refer to household pets; in the Scriptures, they are wild, unclean, and often despised (see for example 1 Samuel 17:43). Thus, the injunction not to give to dogs what is sacred and not to throw one's pearls to pigs simply means "do not be undiscerning." If this verse has to do with evangelism, it urges the disciples to be discerning and not to devote their energies in proclaiming the Gospel to those who would reject it with scorn and contempt. This verse provides balance by warning the disciples against becoming undiscerning simpletons!

The importance of a correct interpretation of this passage in the church cannot be over-emphasized. Christians tend to adopt an uncritical posture for fear of being accused of being too judgmental. As a result, a bishop fails to reprimand an errant clergyman; a pastor fails to discipline a member of his congregation; a theologian fails to correct an erroneous teaching. The examples can be multiplied. Here failure is due to fear—the fear of being judged to be judgmental. To repeat, this passage makes the distinction between exercising judgment and being judgmental. It is the responsibility of every Christian to exercise moral and theological judgment based on God's Word. And in our world, the call for Christians to be discerning, to exercise judgment, can never be more urgent. Indeed we should not only pray that every Christian would have a discerning mind, but that she or he might also have the courage to speak the truth in love. Courage without discernment is foolhardiness; but discernment without courage is cowardice. Both foolhardiness and cowardice lead to irresponsible action. Far from condemning all forms of judgment, this passage affirms discernment as a desirable quality in a disciple of Christ. It is the hypocritical, malicious, and haughty sense of moral superiority that it censors and condemns.

Ask, Seek and Knock (Matthew 7: 7-12)

In this passage in the Sermon on the Mount, Jesus assures his disciples that their prayers will be heard and answered according to God's love and faithfulness. Some scholars have tried to demonstrate the connection between this passage and the preceding verses (7:1-6) by extrapolating that Jesus is here teaching that, rather than judging, it is better to ask God to remove the speck in the other person's eye. This interpretation has engendered an attitude that wrongly elevates prayer over criticism, even if the latter is made prayerfully and lovingly. It is hoped that the discussion of the preceding verses would help us to understand why this interpretation is untenable. The statements in this passage are of a piece with Jesus' teaching on prayer in the Sermon. The Sermon began with the acknowledgement of the disciple's bankruptcy before God (5:3). It then provides the model for prayer (6:9-13), and now it provides the assurance that the prayers of the disciples will be heard by God, who will answer them according to his will.

This passage begins with three imperatives: ask, seek, and knock. They refer to the same activity, namely prayer. The imperatives encourage the disciples of Christ to pray; and, with each imperative, success is assured. Hence "Ask and it *shall* be given to you; seek and you *shall* find; knock and the door *will* be opened to you." In v. 8 they are symmetrically repeated. The object is not specified: the disciples were not told what to ask, what to seek, or that for which they knock. Verse 11 suggests that the object of prayer is "good gifts," although it does not describe what they are. Verses 9-11 seem to indicate that the requests have to do with food—that is, with daily sustenance. The present tense in these verses conveys the idea of persistence—the disciples are to continue asking, seeking, and knocking. The passive verbs in vv. 7 and 8 point to the faithfulness of God—God is the one who will answer and open the door. The emphasis here is not the content of the petitions—the "good gifts"— but the faithfulness of God.

The assurance that this passage offers that those who ask will be given what they ask for has sometimes resulted in misconceptions about prayer. A superficial reading of this passage may give the impression that by this promise God *must* answer all our prayers according to our requests. When reality presents a very different picture, disillusionment will no doubt result. Explanatory strategies are then devised to provide the reason why petitions are not answered. The usual reason given is that the person who made them did not have sufficient faith. Bad theology is often the result of wrong exegesis! The rhetorical questions in vv. 9-11 will help clarify the meaning of this passage. "Which of you, if his son asks for bread, will give him a stone? Or if he asks for fish, will give him a snake?" The answer to these questions is, of course, that none of them would. The point is made in v. 11: "If you, then, though you are evil, know how to give good gifts to your children, how much more will your Father in heaven give good gifts to those who ask him!"

The logic here is impeccable. The sinfulness of human parents—and scripture presupposes the moral degradation of the human family—is compared to righteousness and goodness of the Father who is in heaven. People are evil. They are self centered and their desires are perverted. Yet, they are able to give good gifts to their children—they will not give their children a stone when they ask for bread. How much more will the heavenly Father, who is pure goodness, give good gifts to those who ask? Again the emphasis here is not the content of the petition, but the wisdom and goodness of the Father. The Father alone knows what is good for us; and he will always give us good gifts. We, on the other hand, may not know what is good for us. We are short-sighted and self-centered, and our perspective of reality is distorted by our personal prejudices and biases. As a result, what we think is good for us and for our families may not in fact be good. The disciples of Christ, it is true, are commanded to ask, seek, and knock. But they are to do so with the knowledge that their Father in heaven knows what is good for them and the trust that he will give them good gifts.

These statements, therefore, speak of prayer in the context of relationship. Prayer is not magic or a technique. There is no formula for effective prayer, no steps to take or special exercises to do. It is amazing that much of the literature on prayer actually has no sound theology of prayer! Devoid of a proper theology, prayer becomes a technique that one can master. Scripture does not give us a formula for effective prayer. As we have already seen, even the Lord's Prayer provides no formula, only a model. In Scripture, prayer is always placed within the context of a relationship. Outside that context, prayer becomes "occultic" and has to do with the harnessing and manipulation of spiritual powers. In this passage, the context of prayer is the covenantal relationship between God and man. The confidence of prayer is the wisdom and love of the heavenly Father. And the attitude of prayer is that of trusting surrender to the One who is faithful and who gives good gifts.

Verse 12 articulates what is often called the "Golden Rule." The Golden Rule was not invented by Jesus, but was found in many different contexts. Some readers may know the story of Rabbi Hillel. In AD 20, he was challenged by a Gentile to summarize the Law in the short time that the Gentile can stand on one leg. Hillel responded by saying: "What is hateful to you, do not do to anyone else. This is the whole law; all the rest is commentary." The Golden Rule can be said to be the exegesis of Leviticus 19:18, "You shall love your neighbor as yourself." Elsewhere in the Gospel of Matthew (22:35-40), Jesus articulated the two greatest commandments on the basis of Deuteronomy 6:5 and Leviticus 19:18. To "love your neighbor as yourself" is equivalent to doing to others what you would have them do to you. The emphasis here is to be found in the emphatic "in everything." This rule applies to every aspect of the life of the disciple and touches all relationships. It summarizes the Law and the Prophets, and its scope is unlimited.

But the Golden Rule also encapsulates the heart of the Sermon on the Mount. It is the essence of all of Jesus' ethical teaching in the Sermon, whether that has to do with judging others or loving one's enemies. The adverb with which the verse begins ("So") brings this out clearly. It refers to the entire body of the Sermon so far (5:17—7:12). "So," in the light of all that I have taught about the essence of the Law, obey the Golden Rule, for it sums up the Law and the Prophets. Thus, the Golden Rule cannot be reduced to some utilitarian maxim like "Honesty is the best policy." It brings to expression the teaching of the Law and the Prophets, and therefore is the expression of the will of God. The disciples of Christ abide by this rule, not because they expect others to do the same to them, but unconditionally, because it is the command of God.

CHAPTER EIGHT

Sure Foundation

The Narrow Gate of Salvation (Matthew 7:13-14)

THE SERMON on the Mount ends with four warnings, each presented by a pair of contrasts. Jesus' audience, which includes his disciples, have to choose between two ways (vv. 13-14), two trees (vv. 15-20), two claims (vv. 21-23), and two builders (vv. 24-27). Their choice will have serious implications on their relationship to the kingdom of God about which Jesus has been speaking. The first pair of contrasts has to do with two ways leading up to two gates. The first gate is narrow and the second gate is broad. Of course, the gate and road here are to be taken metaphorically. The narrow gate points to the difficulty of this way. Although a spatial metaphor is used here, the intention is to refer to the difficult demands of Christian discipleship and the persecution that those who belong to Christ must endure. Jesus warned his disciples that the way to the kingdom is difficult and unattractive, and he later predicted that only a few would take it. But those who do will receive eternal life, that is, life in the eternal presence of God.

The second, more popular way is the broad road that leads to the wide gate. Again, the metaphors are spatial, and they imply the ease and comfort of those who chose this way. Those who walk this way will not be met by any significant demands to order their lives according to the ethical precepts that Jesus has explained in the Sermon. They do not need to bother with discipline or with obedience to God's Word. They are free to live their lives as they please, free to have other allegiances, free to abandon themselves to their lusts and desires. This way is surely more attractive, and there are indeed many who will take it. But this way leads to ruin. If entry by the narrow gate brings life, entry by this broad gate brings destruction. And the word for destruction refers to that which is definitive: eternal separation from God. Thus, the two roads are not ends in themselves, but lead to two distinct and opposite destinations. Thus, there are two roads, two gates, two crowds, two destinations.

The passage suggests that choice of the way to either life or destruction has already begun in the here and now, although there is a reference to the future. Those who have chosen to walk the narrow road and enter the narrow gate have already received life in the here and now, and those who have chosen the opposite route are already condemned. The idea of the immediacy of salvation or judgment is clearly found in the Gospel of John. In John 5:24 we are told that those who have placed their faith in Jesus Christ *have already passed from death to life*. In the same way, those who have rejected him are already condemned. The eschatological judgment has already begun to take effect in the here and now (John 3:18; 9:39; 12:47).

The passage also makes clear that Jesus did not come to judge but to save. His coming has made the road to salvation possible, even though Christian discipleship and obedience in this world of sin and contradiction is never easy. This truth is made explicit in John 3:17: "For God did not send his Son into the world to condemn the world, but to save the world through him." This verse states that the supreme reason for the Incarnation—the coming of the Son of God in human flesh—is salvation. But how can this be reconciled with John 5:22, which says that the Father has given "all judgment to the Son"?

To be sure, scripture teaches that the Son has come to save and therefore judges no one. But the Word that he speaks will bring judgment. Those who reject his Word and, as a consequence, also reject his gift of salvation, have therefore brought judgment upon themselves: "For I did not come to judge the world, but to save it. There is a judge for the one who rejects me and does not accept my words; *that very word which I spoke will condemn him at the last day*" (John 12:47-8). Although the Savior made no judicial decision, some decision has nevertheless taken place. Those who choose to reject the Son of God are judged and condemned by the Word that he has spoken.

The concepts of hell and eternal damnation have become very unpopular in modern culture. Modern man finds the idea of a God who assigns those who refuse his friendship to eternal punishment repulsive, especially in the wake of the horrors and atrocities of concentration camps. It is impossible to think of a God who would condemn unbelievers to endless suffering in an eternal Auschwitz. Those in earthly concentration camps can at least hope for an ultimate deliverance—death—if escape or release has proved impossible. But those in hell will suffer for all eternity without any hope of emancipation. Furthermore, the doctrine of eternal punishment in hell, it is argued, cannot really fit into the Biblical concept of the God of love. For moderns, then, eternal punishment is inimical to the Biblical portrayal of a loving God.

For some, the solution to this so-called problem is found in the concept of universal salvation. Those who hold this view (universalism) reject the idea that God will banish people to eternal punishment in hell because it is God's will that everyone should be saved. The concepts of eternal punishment and hell belong to a medieval notion of God that is fashioned after archaic notions of justice and punishment and therefore cannot be a part of Christianity that preaches the Gospel of the love of God. Some universalists meet the objection that the Bible speaks explicitly of hell by arguing that hell is real from the point of view of the person making the decision, but ultimately it is an impossibility for God. As universalist John A. T. Robinson puts it: "In a universe of love there can be no heaven which tolerates a chamber of horrors." Hell, therefore, becomes a psychological rather than a metaphysical reality. Finally, universalists argue that the reality of hell contradicts the sovereignty of God. For if the God who wills that all should be saved is truly sovereign, then the universal salvation of human beings will surely in the end be realized.

Space does not allow a detailed response to universalism. Suffice it is to say that in this passage Jesus makes it very clear that there are two possible destinations for all human beings. The love of God does not negate human freedom, and God's offer of love can either be embraced or spurned by his rational creatures. Universalism works on an erroneous idea of omnipotence, because it insists that divine sovereignty will in the end negate human freedom—those who continue to reject God will be forced in his presence against their will. Universalism, therefore, works on the same notion of divine sovereignty as the doctrine of double predestination that it rejects. Furthermore, universalism fails to take seriously the human sin that sent the Son of God to Calvary's Cross . The Cross and resurrection of Christ are made available to all, but only those who believe in the Son of God will appropriate them. Although the Bible teaches that salvation is universally accessible, it does not teach universal salvation.

This passage brings out the creative tension between divine grace and human freedom. The grace of God has opened the way to salvation, but it is through the exercise of their God-given freedom that human beings appropriate this salvation. The grace of God is persuasive, not coercive. It honors human freedom and invites human beings to receive God's gift of salvation out of their own volition. God invites sinful human beings to enter into a covenantal relationship with him, but he never forces humans into that relationship. In fact, it could be said that God never really sends anyone to hell. The negative outcome of his offer of salvation comes about because of the individual's rejection of that offer. Destruction is the destination of those who choose to reject the offer of life and choose instead to enter through the broad gate.

A Tree and Its Fruit (Matthew 7:15-23)

In this passage Jesus uses the metaphors of trees and fruits to describe genuine discipleship. There are two types of trees that bear two different types of fruits. "Bad tree" represents the false prophets, while "good tree" represents the disciples of Christ. The passage begins with a serious warning to "watch out for false prophets." That special discernment is needed to identify them is indicated by the statement that these prophets come "in sheep's clothing" that camouflages their real intentions and disguises their true nature, namely, that of "ferocious wolves." These false prophets pretend to be part of the people of God and teachers of the truth, when, in fact, they are deceivers, whose purpose is to lead the people of God astray (Matthew 24:24). They masquerade as teachers of the Word of God, claiming to have special and profound insights into the mind of God and the divine plan, when, in fact, they are merely presenting their own delusional ideas and ideals. They claim to be servants of the most-high God, when, in fact, they are slaves of their own insatiable egos.

While detection is made difficult because of their disguise in sheep's clothing, it is not impossible. "By their fruit you will recognize them," Jesus said. "Fruit" refers to the conduct or behavior of these prophets. False prophets may dazzle their audience with eloquence and profundity, but their behavior will betray their real intentions and their true motivations. Like produces like, and evil comes from evil. The outside camouflage cannot for long disguise the true characters of these prophets, and what is inside will surface, for a false face cannot hide a false heart—at least, not for very long! "Fruit," therefore, refers to the total life and character of a person. Good fruit has to do with Christlike qualities like meekness, gentleness, love, patience, kindness, goodness, etc. When a prophet fails to exhibit these qualities, when he instead shows enmity, impurity, jealousy, self-indulgence, and pride, there is reason to be suspicious of his intentions.

But "fruit" also has to do with the content of the prophet's teaching. John Calvin clearly saw that and judged that those who "confine them [fruits] to the life [conduct]" were mistaken. Fruit here refers to the man's actual teaching, the content of his doctrine, his theology. The fact that teaching can be false means that Christian doctrine is not some vacuous linguistic game, but that it has to do with the Truth. The Church has always held this, as the history of theology testifies. Christian doctrine is not a matter of the opinion of individuals or a group of individuals. Neither is Christian doctrine merely the meaningful regulatory discourse of the Christian community. Christian doctrine deals with truths about God and the world that are made known by God's revelation. The presence of heresies implies that these truths can be and have been distorted, and corrupt and erroneous traditions can develop within the Church. The demand of Christian discipleship has to do not only with right living, but also *right thinking* and *right understanding*. Jesus warned against false prophets because truth is objective, doctrine is not a matter of individual opinion and conviction, and doctrinal decisions cannot be made democratically.

Theological relativism is alive and well in both liberal and evangelical sectors of the Protestant Church. In liberal circles, Christian doctrine is swallowed up by cultural relativism, in which the changing cultural sensibilities will determine the way in which the tenets of the faith are interpreted. In evangelical circles, especially those influenced by pietism, theological relativism comes through the idea of "conviction" that is shaped by individualism. "This is my conviction; this is my belief; this is what the Lord told me to do." This idea of conviction is utterly subjective and relativistic, anchored not on the solid rock of God's Word, but the shifting sands of our emotional and psychological states. In this age of relativism, heresies and heretics have all but disappeared. Once truth is subjectivized, and a more accommodative spirit is encouraged, the church's sense of discernment is numbed and her organ for distinguishing truth from falsehood is impaired. The Church must take the warning of Jesus in these verses seriously if she is to be prevented from being deceived.

In his Olivet discourse, Jesus warned his hearers that there would be a proliferation of false teachings in the "last days." These false teachers will, with eloquence and charisma, deceive the people, even the elect. They will appear and perform great signs and miracles (Matthew 24:24) that will bedazzle the less discerning in the Christian community. They will have a pre-occupation with prophecies regarding the end of the age and the consummation of the kingdom of God and will make predictions regarding the return of Christ. The history of the Church offers many examples of such "prophets." And they will continue to multiply in our time, especially in the wake of prevailing uncertainties and gloom. They will come from within the Church and will be of fundamentalist as well as liberal persuasions. They will come wearing glamorous and attractive outward clothing, to use the metaphor again, in their charming eloquence and with their academic and ecclesiastical credentials. This passage reminds us that prophets are to be judged by their fruits—by their conduct and teaching—rather than by their academic and ecclesiastical accolades. This passage tells us that it is naïve to think that, just because a person is a Ph.D. or a D.D., a professor, a clergyman, or a bishop, he or she is a true teacher of the Word of God.

Verses 21-23 are surely, for some, the most difficult in this passage. "Not everyone who says to me, 'Lord, Lord,' will enter the kingdom of heaven": not even those who prophesy in the name of Lord or those who exorcize in his Name or perform many miracles in his Name. These are not only people who confessed Christ, but also those who were endowed with charisma and were involved in spectacular ministries. They are evangelists, preachers, and miracle workers. Yet confession and charisma will not guarantee their entry into the kingdom of God. What are we to make of this passage? What is the point that Jesus was trying to make here?

The emphasis of this passage is made clear in the contrasting clause in the second half of v. 21. Entry into the kingdom of God is allowed only to those who do the will of the Father who is in heaven. This is the emphasis of the entire Sermon on the Mount, which makes it clear that it is more important to be obedient to the will of God than to perform religious rituals. Here, the stress is that obedience is far more important than verbal confessions and possessing certain charismata. Like every passage in the Sermon, this passage forces us to go deeper than the surface, to penetrate into the heart of the matter, to the very seat of the motivations of man. This passage is not saying that confession is unimportant, but that without the commitment of obedience, such confession is vacuous. Similarly, this passage is not criticizing charismatic activities, but warns that they can never replace obedience and that if they are done because of selfish motivations, they have no self-contained importance.

Two Builders (Matthew 7:24-29)

We come to the final passage in the Sermon on the Mount. Here Jesus describes two builders who went about the business of building houses for themselves. It goes without saying that Jesus is using parabolic language to describe two significantly different types of people, although their difference is at first difficult to detect. The similarities between them may be seen in the fact that they both had drive and purpose. Even after they have completed their building projects, they both appeared, initially at least, to have succeeded. On the surface, it is very difficult to detect any difference in their handiwork. Both houses appear to be well built and sturdy. The external features do not reveal the real condition of the houses. This links this parable to a central theme in the Sermon on the Mount: there is more to spirituality than meets the eye. If external appearances truly reflect the spiritual well-being and authenticity of a person, then the Pharisees would be spiritual giants!

This parable impresses upon us the great truth that foundations are everything. The foolish person, according to this parable, is the one who would build directly on sand, which provides no protection against the devastation of the elements. The wise person living in the Palestinian desert, however, would choose to build upon the rock, a solid and secure foundation that he knows will protect the house from floods and sudden storms. Jesus then speaks of the testing that will come, because any building must face the vicissitudes of its useful life. And it is then when the truth about the buildings, their fundamental difference is revealed. The rain, flood, and wind are, according to some scholars, symbols of the final Day of Judgment, during which all will be revealed. The eschatological nature of the Sermon on the Mount makes this interpretation attractive, although these metaphors may also refer to calamities that are experienced in life that would test the authenticity of one's faith. As the storm breaks and the houses are subjected to severe battering, the truth about the buildings, their fundamental and fatal difference, is finally revealed. The house built upon solid rock withstood the rain, flood, and gale. But the one built on sand collapsed in irreparable ruin. Truth will out when difficulties and challenges confront the person who calls himself or herself a Christian.

The parable makes it very clear that hearing the Word of God alone is not enough. A thorough knowledge of Scripture is, of course, important. But without obedience, such knowledge alone will not save us from ruin when the storms of life come. Scripture repeatedly emphasizes the importance of being an obedient doer of God's Word. In Matthew 12:50, Jesus points out that obedience is vitally important to our relationship with him: "For whoever does the will of my Father in heaven is my brother and sister and mother." And classically in James 1:22-25, the apostle emphasizes that true discipleship takes place only when there is a correlation between hearing and doing God's Word. It is this central theme—obedience—that properly conjoins 7:15-23 and 7:24-27. Just as mere profession of the lordship of Christ (v. 21) and ministerial competence (vv. 22-23) are insufficient to ascertain the authenticity of one's commitment, so too is the knowledge of God's Word an insufficient gauge of discipleship.

This passage makes it quite clear that faith and obedience are profoundly and inextricably related. The builder who builds his house upon sand is not someone with a weak faith. The passage suggests that such a person has no faith at all! The person who simply hears the Word of Christ but does not obey does not have faith in Christ, because obedience is not an added extra; obedience is the evidence of faith. Thus we may say that *only the believers obey*, and *only the obedient believe*. The one statement cannot be understood without the other. The first statement is easy enough to understand. Only believers obey. This means that faith is the pre-requisite of obedience, and obedience is the manifestation—the making evident—of faith. The second statement makes it clear that obedience is that which prevents faith from becoming a form of self-deception. Only those who put to practice the word of Christ has truly made faith real by obedience. As Bonhoeffer has so eloquently put it, "A concrete commandment has to be obeyed, in order to come to believe." The fact remains that the disobedient cannot have faith. The disobedient cannot believe: only the obedient believe.

Matthew brings this long discourse to a close by emphasizing the authority of the speaker. "The crowds were amazed" at the teachings of Jesus. Why were they amazed? Was it because Jesus had given them insights that are totally new and unique? This cannot be the case, because at least some aspects the teaching of the Sermon on the Mount can be found in other religious and cultural contexts. Verse 29 makes it clear that Jesus' audience was amazed at his teaching because "he taught as one who had authority." This assessment must be understood theologically. By this statement Matthew is not content to say that Jesus was just a brilliant moral teacher, even the moral teacher *par excellence*. This, indeed, is the verdict of numerous contemporary readers of the Sermon of the Mount. They will go so far as to say that Jesus of Nazareth was perhaps the greatest moral teacher who ever lived. But for Matthew, this assertion has not gone far enough. For him, Jesus' authority is different from that of the teachers of the law, because Jesus is the incarnate Word of God. We return at the end to the statements that prefaced this series of expositions: that the Sermon on the Mount cannot be interpreted without christology. The Sermon on the Mount can only be understood in the light of the person of the Preacher. Understood in this way, the Sermon can never be merely a piece of fine ethics. It is a divine call; a divine call that is made on all of us. For the Sermon is not merely the words of a man, not even those of a very great man. It is the Word of God.

Select Bibliography

Bonhoeffer, Dietrich. *Discipleship*. Edited by Geffrey B. Kelly and John D. Godsey. Translated by Barbara Green and Reinhard Krauss. Dietrich Bonhoeffer Works 4. Minneapolis: Fortress, 2001.
Carson, D. A. *Jesus' The Sermon on the Mount and His Confrontation with the World: An Exposition of Matthew 5–10*. 1978. Reprinted, Eugene, Ore.: Wipf & Stock, 2004.
Gore, Charles. *The Sermon on the Mount: A Practical Exposition*. London: Murray, 1899.
Hughes, Kent. *The Sermon on the Mount: The Message of the Kingdom*. Leicester, Eng.: Crossway, 2001.
Lloyd Jones, D. Martyn. *Studies on the Sermon on the Mount*. 2 vols. London: InterVarsity Fellowship, 1959–60.
Luther, Martin. *The Sermon on the Mount and the Magnificat*. Luther's Works 21. St Louis: Concordia, 1956.
Palmer, Earl F. *The Enormous Exception: Meeting Christ in the Sermon on the Mount*. Waco, Tex.: Word, 1986.
John Paul II, Pope. *Blessed Are the Pure in Heart: Catechism on the Sermon on the Mount and the Writings of Paul*. Boston: St. Paul Books and Media, 1983.
Stassen, Glen H., and David P. Gushee. *Kingdom Ethics: Following Jesus in Contemporary Context*. Downers Grove, Ill.: InterVarsity, 2003.
Stott, John. *The Message of the Sermon on the Mount (Matthew 5–7): Christian Counter-Culture*. Downers Grove, Ill.: InterVarsity, 1978.
Thielicke, Helmut. *Life Can Begin Again: Sermons on the Sermon on the Mount*. Translated by John W. Doberstein. 1963. Reprinted, Eugene, Ore.: Wipf & Stock, 2003.
Thurneysen, Eduard. *Sermon on the Mount*. Translated by William Childs Robinson Sr. with James M. Robinson. Richmond: John Knox, 1964.

www.ingramcontent.com/pod-product-compliance
Lightning Source LLC
Chambersburg PA
CBHW050840160426
43192CB00011B/2093